Joined-up Youth Justice

Tackling Youth Crime in Partnership

Ros Burnett

and

Catherine Appleton

LEARNING RESOURCES
CENTRE

Havering College
of Further and Higher Education

RHP

Russell House Publishing

First published in 2004 by:
Russell House Publishing Ltd.
4 St George's House
Uplyme Road
Lyme Regis
Dorset D17 3LS

Tel: 01297-443948
Fax: 01297-442722
e-mail: help@russellhouse.co.uk
www.russellhouse.co.uk

British Library Cataloguing-in-publication Data:
A catalogue record for this book is available from the British Library

ISBN: 1-903855-32-2

Typeset by GCS, Leighton Buzzard, Beds.

Printed by Antony Rowe, Chippenham

About Russell House Publishing

RHP is a group of social work, probation, education and youth and community work practitioners and academics working in collaboration with a professional publishing team.

Our aim is to work closely with the field to produce innovative and valuable materials to help managers, trainers, practitioners and students.

We are keen to receive feedback on publications and new ideas for future projects.

For details of our other publications please visit our website or ask us for a catalogue. Contact details are on this page.

Contents

Acknowledgements

The research on which this book is based was commissioned by the Oxfordshire Youth Offending Team and funded indirectly by the Youth Justice Board via development funding to the Oxfordshire County Council. Undertaking the research, and then writing the book, required the co-operation and support of a large number of people.

First and foremost, we are grateful to Maggie Blyth, the first YOT Manager, Mike Simm, the present Head of Youth Offending Services and Steve Crocker, Deputy Manager, and all the practitioners in the team, for letting us 'in' on the experience of setting up and developing their joined-up youth justice service. For two and a half years, they accepted without complaint our perpetual presence at meetings as well as our regular appearance in their email inbox in search of that extra bit of information. A special thank you is extended to staff running the partnership projects for sharing their plans and expertise and ensuring that we were kept up to date. Many other people who had no obligation to speak to us, generously did so: magistrates; mentors; victims; parents; and - the main users of the YOT service - young people. This study has benefited greatly from their forthrightness in sharing their views.

Research assistance was provided by Mark Fransham, now a Research Officer at NACRO, who carried out most of the fieldwork in Huntercombe Young Offender Institution, and provided some of the material used in Chapter 7. The interviewing of young people was assisted by a team of fieldworkers. We thank them for the interviews that they managed to carry out and for endeavouring to achieve more - in particular Christine McCullach, Danielle Moon, Teela Sanders, Tina Andersen Huey and Gill Walker, whose persistence paid off.

We are most grateful to Aidan Wilcox, Martina Feilzer, David Faulkner, Carolyn Hoyle, Richard Young, and other colleagues at the Centre for Criminological Research for helping in various ways. Steve Ballinger, who was then the Administrator to the Centre for Criminological Research, coped cheerfully and efficiently with the additional burden thrown up by the recruitment and administering of part-time interviewers. Professor Roger Hood, then Director of the Centre for Criminological Research, provided welcome advice at critical stages in the life of the project, and we are grateful to both him and Colin Roberts, Head of the Probation Studies Unit, for their generous support.

It has been a great pleasure, in planning this book, to work with Geoffrey Mann, Managing Director of Russell House Publishing, and John Pitts, distinguished academic as well as a commissioning editor for Russell House. We thank them for their patience and constructive advice. Lastly, but by no means least, we thank our respective partners, Peter Burnett and Bent Grøver, and our families for still 'being there' and continuing to believe in us when we were spending too many weekends at work instead of with them.

Ros Burnett
Catherine Appleton
Oxford

Abbreviations

ABC	Acceptable Behaviour Contract
ABH	Actual Bodily Harm
ADHD	Attention Deficit Hyperactivity Disorder
ASBO	Anti-Social Behaviour Order
CAMHS	Child and Adolescent Mental Health Services
CDA	Crime and Disorder Act
DAAT	Drug and Alcohol Team
DNA	Did not attend
DTO	Detention and Training Order
ESW	Education Social Worker
ETE	Education, Training and Employment
ISSP	Intensive Supervision and Surveillance Programme
NACRO	National Association for the Care and Resettlement of Offenders
NHS	National Health Service
OYOT	Oxfordshire Youth Offending Team
PCT	Primary Care Trust
PYO	Persistent Young Offender
YOP	Youth Offender Panel
YIP	Youth Inclusion Programmes
YISP	Youth Inclusion and Support Panels
YJB	Youth Justice Board
YOI	Young Offender Institution
YOIS	Youth Offending Information System
YOT	Youth Offending Team

Figures and Boxes

There is huge commitment and goodwill to this. I don't hear people moaning about the YOT or other aspects of inter-agency work to tackle youth crime. People are really wanting to give it a go, and to look at difficult and seemingly intractable problems to find solutions and make progress. I don't know where that comes from, whether that was part of the culture before, but I certainly see that willingness around the YOT to try and tackle those problems together. In a way you need that cultural ethos as a prerequisite and a starting point.
(Member of the Youth Offending Team Steering Group)

CHAPTER 1
Introduction

The twenty-first century ushered in a revised youth justice system in England and Wales. One of its key characteristics is that it brings together people from numerous professions and agencies as well as volunteers from the community. The victims of crime and the young people who have offended against them, plus representatives of each, are also included in this collective effort to address youth crime. This book is intended for contributors to, and users of, youth justice services, and others who seek an overview of the changes and how they have been implemented. While readers are likely to be experts in one or more of the procedures and services that make up youth justice, they may be less familiar with what other contributors to the system are doing and the issues that concern them. Based on research which took a holistic perspective of the development and delivery of youth justice, the following chapters touch on and inter-link numerous pieces in the jigsaw to enable a view of the 'bigger picture'.

This story of youth justice reform should be particularly meaningful to those who have grappled with the complexities of turning the vision of joined-up services into a working reality. Few are likely to question the ideal of collaborative work, with its implied promise of shared effort and expertise, and shared information between participants, all working towards the same goals. But while the rhetoric is easy, the achievement - involving so many parties with differing objectives, resources and viewpoints - is inevitably a complex process. It has sometimes been pointed out that the term 'system' in 'criminal justice system' is a misnomer because of the detached way in which the different agencies involved have carried out their activities (Cavadino and Dignan, 2002). The reformed services for youth justice do at least merit the label of system given that agencies have joined forces and are carrying out services that are interdependent. Sections in the following pages consider, in turn, the contributions of different agencies and the developmental and practical issues which are involved in achieving a joined-up system.

Most of the examples are drawn from the arrangements in one county, Oxfordshire, which served as an in-depth case study for the research on which this book is based. By focussing mainly on one youth offending team (YOT), and its partnership projects, at different stages of development (planning, setting-up, bedding down) and at all levels of action (strategic, operational management and front-line practice) we were able to gain insight into the whole system and to appraise the working operation of the strategic ideals. As far as we are aware, no other YOT to date has been the subject of a similar in-depth study investigating core practice, strategic and operational management and all of the associated partnership projects.[1] Single case studies can provide rich terrain for detailed understanding of a subject, whereas an aggregate study would not usually permit the same attention to detail (Stake, 2000). Large amounts

---

[1] It should be noted though that the 'pilots' of youth offending teams were subject to a separate evaluation covering most aspects (Holdaway et al., 2001) as were some which were set up early in the shadow of the pilots and so referred to as 'shadow' YOTs (Bailey and Williams, 2000).

of information were collected across a wide range of dimensions. Although Oxfordshire YOT - which we refer to throughout as OYOT - was just one of 154 YOTs set up in the UK, it was one of a small number of YOTs, initially eight, granted 'pathway' status by the Youth Justice Board. As the label implies, 'pathway' YOTs were intended to blaze a trail and to help determine which interventions and methods of delivery worked best to achieve the Board's main aim of reducing offending. OYOT adopted a comprehensive approach in taking up various initiatives and, as a 'pathway' YOT, it attracted above average funding. It was therefore particularly suitable for a case study.

The authors followed the progress of this YOT for nearly two and a half years from before the time of its inception, and this study therefore reflects back on a moving reality. We learned about the process of setting up and delivering services by carrying out well over 400 interviews, collecting and analysing process data, regularly observing and participating in meetings, taking part in staff training events and 'away-days' as well as exchanging communications on a daily basis. In our role as its evaluators we were seen as making a specific contribution alongside other specialist members, and the constancy of our presence meant that, in effect, we became 'participant observers'. We were often referred to as part of the team and whenever the list of team members was updated and circulated, our names were always included.

One of our objectives, in so closely tracking developments from the sidelines, was to observe the difficulties and accomplishments of this endeavour with a view to sharing the insights gained. The period of the study covered distinct stages of the YOT's developments as it formed and changed shape. In its first two years it grew in size from about 35 members of staff to over 70 staff, in addition to 40 sessional workers and 50 volunteers. Clearly, further changes will have taken place since the period of our involvement and some of the problems noted were the inevitable difficulties of a new system which are likely to have since been resolved. The examples given however remain valid as illustrations of the issues involved in establishing and delivering the reforms. While we have focussed mainly on the experiences of one local youth justice service, we have done so in order to explore issues which are likely to resonate for others. Our goal is to provide breadth of coverage, overview and practical insight for those who want to get on with the task of delivering 'joined-up' youth justice.

In Chapter 1 we introduce the present youth justice system brought in by the Crime and Disorder Act 1998 and the Youth Justice and Criminal Evidence Act 1999. In order to contrast old and new systems and to provide basic background information, the chapter begins with a backward look at legislation during the twentieth century to deal with offending by children and young people. Chapter 2 addresses strategic management issues in setting up this partnership approach to youth offending. In Chapter 3 the work of practitioners as case holders, case managers, deliverers of pre-court interventions and officers responsible for delivering court orders is discussed.

Chapter 4 explores those elements of the new approach which are aimed at first and second offences (reprimands and final warnings) or first court appearances (referral orders). The common elements here are that these disposals are aimed at the early stages of offending; both involve meetings to discuss the offence and appropriate responses; and both give emphasis to the victim perspective and are informed by restorative justice principles. Chapter 5 is focussed on the role of the youth court and the use of legislation available for sentencing young offenders. We describe individual court orders and their use, with particular reference to the views of magistrates and YOT officers. In Chapter 6 we describe and analyse the application of a range of specialist interventions and programmes that have been developed to address problems associated with youth offending including: mentoring; parenting; substance abuse; basic skills; mental health; careers; and offending behaviour projects.

In Chapter 7 we turn to sentences at the 'heavy end' - that is, custodial sentences and intensive supervision and surveillance. We look at the practical issues and risks raised by the imprisonment of children and young people, and consider the inter-relationship between the work of YOT staff and YOI staff in the delivery of Detention and Training Orders. Chapter 8 assesses what has been achieved in meeting the objectives set by the Youth Justice Board. The final chapter summarises the main findings and lessons learned, and provides recommendations for more efficient and effective delivery of services aimed at reducing offending.

Several academic writers have published provocative critiques lamenting the changes to youth justice and representing the system as repressive and misconceived, notably: Goldson (2000); Muncie (2001); Pitts (2003); and Smith (2003). While the present book will point to problems encountered and various ways in which the developments have been less than perfect, our purpose is not to add to the vitriol. A problem with such critiques is that they can seem to undermine the efforts of people obliged to work within the system being lambasted. A large workforce has had to take on the task of making the changes and trying to make them work. Many accepted them in good faith as relevant to reducing offending and are committed to the principle of reducing offending. The spirit of staff who formed the partnerships and entered into inter-agency arrangements to make this work was mostly constructive and optimistic - as the quotation of the frontispiece illustrates. Such a perspective, in itself, can be expected to be a potent force for positive change. We have therefore chosen to present the findings of this study in the same spirit of constructive optimism. If we can stimulate further thought and discussion about appropriate ways in which partnership projects in general and youth justice in particular can be made to work then the book will have begun to achieve its main objective.

CHAPTER 2

Responding to Youth Crime: Past and Present

In debates about the problem of youth crime, discussants are apt to come forward with what they claim is an obvious solution. Yet one person's view of the incontrovertible way forward is likely to be diametrically opposed to another's suggestion that is proposed with equal certainty. Arguments that 'a good dose of corporal punishment' or 'a spell in the army' would cut crime are poles apart from assertions that ending child poverty is the essential way to address the problem. If the solution is so self-evident then why are firmly held opinions so at odds with each other? Such clashing viewpoints cannot be dismissed as held only by the uninformed: these polarities of opinion are equally to be found among criminal justice professionals, lawyers, academics and politicians as well as armchair criminologists. Maybe resolving the problem of youth crime is not so straightforward.

The nature of the problem

Shifts in penal policy for offending by juveniles and adolescents have mirrored to some extent alternative perspectives on the causes of youth crime as, on the one hand, a normal part of growing up and, on the other hand, as the behaviour of maladjusted, dysfunctional individuals who are out of control. Two decades ago, West concluded that: 'Partly as a result of the persistence of these exaggerated and contradictory stereotypes social policies for dealing with youthful delinquency remain in a state of flux and confusion' (1982: 2). Some criminal justice experts would argue that this statement is more applicable than ever. For example, the reformed youth justice system has been referred to as a 'mélange of measures' that reveals 'fundamental contradictions' (Muncie, 2001: 165) and as a 'melting pot of principles and ideologies' (Fionda, 1999: 36).

However, rather than simply being a manifestation of confusion and ambivalence, the mixed approach embedded in the present legislation can be interpreted, at least partly, as an attempt to cater for the heterogeneity of offending and offenders. 'Juvenile delinquency', 'youth crime' and 'anti-social behaviour' are unitary terms that denote plural behaviours for which there are multiple causes and a variety of theoretical explanations. The endless debates could more readily be resolved if, instead of being generally lumped together, different categories of offenders and types of offending were more consistently distinguished.

Academics have contributed to the conflicting messages about youth crime. A dominant criminological perspective is that young people are no more or less delinquent than they have always been, but rather it is media representations and popular perceptions that have changed (Cohen, 1983; Pearson, 1983). Youth justice experts have argued that young people have 'become the legitimate target of any politician or populist commentator who seeks to create an easy scapegoat for the failure of their own ideas and promises' (Haines and Drakeford, 1998: 29) and that fear of youth crime is useful as 'a kind of electoral glue... [that] can bind together an otherwise disparate band of electors... [and] may be used to repair rifts within political parties' (Pitts, 2003: 2). As a counterbalance against unhelpful media and police depictions of young people as 'laughing hyenas', 'rat boys' and other demonic images, scholars have done much to restore a view of youthful misdemeanours as a normal phase of growing-up, best dealt with by minimal intervention from the penal system (Rutherford, 1985). The basis for this position is that adolescence is a period of life that is 'mistake-prone by design', intellectual capacities and powers of reasoning are still developing, and young people learn by doing and from making mistakes (Zimring, 2000: 283). Such immaturity suggests that youth might be regarded as a 'mitigating factor' even though they should be held culpable to some extent (von Hirsch, 2001).

Crime statistics and surveys on the extent of crime have not helped to clear up alternative messages about the growth and seriousness of youth crime. Official statistics show a clear rise in overall crime rates over the last 50 years and it is estimated that at least a quarter of recorded crime is committed by 10-17 year olds (Farrington, 1996; Home Office, 1995; Rutter et al., 1998). A problem with official statistics is that they may reflect changes in judicial and policing practices rather than 'real' crime trends. A detailed analysis of juvenile crime trends in West European countries from 1950 to the mid-1990s was carried out by Estrada (1999) which made use of alternative sources of data (including self-report victim surveys) in addition to crime statistics. This showed that, rather than a continuous upward trend in juvenile crime in the post-war period 1950-1995, there had been an initial increase followed by a levelling-off in most European countries since the mid-1970s. Exceptions to this pattern, however, were found for England, Germany and, more questionably, Finland: in each of these countries the rise in youth crime continued. In England there was a downturn in *recorded* juvenile crime rates in the late 1980s, but a study by Farrington (1992) suggested that this reflected changes in official reactions, such as police procedures in implementing the Police and Criminal Evidence Act, rather than a decline in offending. The latest crime statistics (adult as well as juvenile) for England and Wales are more encouraging. According to the *British Crime Survey* (BCS), which is based on self-reports of the crime which people have experienced, there has been a 25 per cent fall in crime in the five years between 1997 and 2002/03 (Simmons and Dodd, 2003). Such figures, however, do not tell us anything about the age of offenders.

Whether youth crime has risen, levelled or fallen in more recent years, no-one disputes that the last half century saw dramatic rises. Over the same period, psychosocial disorders among young people (including alcohol abuse, drug abuse, depression, suicide) rose steeply (Rutter et al., 1998). The incidence of such psychological disorders has been found to be high among *persistent* young offenders. A review of relevant research found that persistent young offenders compared to other young people have more educational problems, more disrupted and impoverished family backgrounds, more experiences of institutional care, lower levels of social integration, more developmental difficulties including hyperactivity (Rutter et al., 1998). Such findings indicate that offending behaviour in many of these cases is dysfunctional rather than a normal part of growing up.

While numerous self-report surveys have shown the normality of offending, especially among boys and young men, it is also well-substantiated by research that a small percentage of offenders are responsible for a high proportion of crime. A recent Home Office survey of youth crime based on the self-reports of 4,848 people aged between 12 and 30 years found that ten per cent of those who reported offending were responsible for nearly half the crimes admitted by the sample (Flood-Page et al., 2000). The two images of the young offender - as, on the one hand, going through a typical stage of adolescent development and, on the other hand, as disadvantaged and dysfunctional - are therefore both applicable to large segments of the young offender population, though with widely differing implications for penal policy. While we can treat offending behaviour as on a continuum given the very high level of law-breaking admitted by the general population, it is helpful to distinguish some sub-groups along this continuum. Rutter and colleagues suggest that sub-groups based on critical variables, such as early onset of anti-social behaviour, and early hyperactivity, have been linked to persistent and serious offending. Complementary to this, a helpful distinction has been made between 'adolescent-limited' and 'life-course persistent' anti-social behaviour (Moffitt, 1993).

Previous responses to youth crime

A brief look backwards at historical responses to youth crime in England and Wales (and in the USA) shows continuing vacillation between perspectives on the right way to deal with young people who offend. Sometimes policies have appeared to swing from one extreme to another, and a favourite metaphor used by commentators is that of a pendulum (e.g. Smith, 2003). Similar shifts and cycles of policy have taken place in other European countries and in the USA. The key developments and changes in England and Wales can be summarised most straightforwardly in a chronological chart (see Box 1).

Box 1: Key developments in youth justice up to 1997

1907 Probation of Offenders Act - Juvenile offenders should be supervised in the community. This had already been happening informally.

1908 Children Act - Introduced separate juvenile courts. Juvenile offenders were to be kept separate from adult offenders and treated differently, and parents made responsible. No imprisonment for juveniles under age 14.

1908 Crime Prevention Act - Borstals were introduced - i.e. specialist custodial institutions for juveniles, with regimes of activities, discipline and training.

1933 Children and Young Persons Act - Required courts to 'have regard to the welfare of the child or young person and...in a proper case take steps for securing that provision is made for his education and training' (s.44:1).

1948 Criminal Justice Act - Abolished corporal punishment, and introduced detention centres (for 'short, sharp shock' deterrent sentences).

1969 Children and Young Persons Act - (only partly implemented). Magistrates had to be specifically qualified to sit on a 'juvenile panel' and to deal with juveniles (aged 14-16) whose welfare was to be the prime consideration. Introduced the concept of 'intermediate treatment' - additional activities required by a supervision order as an intermediate measure to avoid removing them from home. No child under the age of 14 to be prosecuted, except for murder. Younger children to be dealt with by civil proceedings.

1977 Criminal Law Act - Increased the powers of juvenile court magistrates to specify what should happen to those they sentenced and to enforce the court orders they made.

1982 Criminal Justice Act - Revived the idea of the 'short, sharp shock' sentences in tough army-style detention centres. Abolished imprisonment for under-21s and transformed the indeterminate borstal sentence into a new, fixed length, order for 'youth custody'.

1983 DHSS Intermediate Treatment Initiative - A programme of seed-corn monies from the Department of Health and Social Services to develop 'intermediate treatment' as an alternative to custody.

1988 Criminal Justice Act - Created a new generic sentence of 'detention in a young offenders institution'. Detention Centres and youth offender institutions all became YOIs.

1989 Children Act - Emphasised the need for the court or local authority to put children first when making decisions and stated that children should be brought up in their own family whenever possible.

1991 Criminal Justice Act - Introduced the principle of proportionate sentencing, thereby formalising notions of 'just deserts'. Juvenile courts were renamed as 'youth courts'.

1997 Crime (Sentences) Act - Extended the discretion of courts to allow names of juveniles to be published.

A fresh start

The title of the 1997 White Paper, *No More Excuses*, sums up the change in strategy and ethos brought in by the Crime and Disorder Act 1998. Whereas the guiding strategy for youth justice practitioners throughout the previous decades had been, above all else, to safeguard the welfare of children and young people, and to divert them from the criminal justice system as far as possible, the new approach was, above all else, aimed at reducing youth offending. It was also to be an interventionist strategy which would bring services and resources together to tackle the risk factors that might lead to further crime.

Research findings had shown that the previous policy of diverting young people from the criminal justice system via the liberal use of cautioning had been followed by lower crime rates among young people (Goldson, 2000). However, considerable media attention given to offending by young people increased public consciousness of youth crime and a sense that policies were not working. A review by the Audit Commission, *Misspent Youth*, attributed apparent reductions in youth crime during the previous decade to demographic change and various 'system effects' in the processing of cases, and suggested that 'once these factors have been taken into account, the rate of offending by young people identified by the police does not appear to have declined' (Audit Commission, 1996: 12). The review concluded that arrangements for dealing with youth offenders were inefficient and expensive. Referring to an audit of criminal justice in Milton Keynes (Shapland et al., 1995), it noted the high cost of successful prosecution, and contrasted this with the economy of 'caution plus' schemes such as those used by the Northamptonshire Diversion Unit and the HALT scheme in Holland (Audit Commission, 1996). Reforms to youth justice were therefore put forward as a pragmatic response to high costs as well as, what was held to be, previous failures in reducing youth crime.

The Crime and Disorder Act 1998, which reflected many recommendations in the Audit Commission Review, marked the beginning of an optimistic fresh start. In the first Annual Report of the Youth Justice Board, its then Chairman, Lord Warner, stated that the Board was 'drawing a line under the past and the failures of the old system' (YJB, 1999: 4). In the discussions which accompanied and followed the reforms brought in by the Crime and Disorder Act, the system was described as 'the *new* youth justice' (Goldson, 2000). What was new? The circularity of approaches during the history of youth justice meant that many aspects had echoes with the past, and most of the elements associated with this fresh start were already in the making or had forerunners in some areas. But the following are elements that characterise post-1997 youth justice.

The United Nations Convention on Human Rights and the Human Rights Act 2000 hold that youth justice services should be accountable for the *welfare* of young people. Some commentators maintain that 'the central purpose of a youth justice service ought to be to do good on behalf of some of the most disadvantaged and distressed young people in the land' (Drakeford, 2001). Moving away from an explicit focus on 'welfare' and helping disadvantaged youngsters, the new youth justice system put the emphasis squarely on reducing re-offending, and this was clearly specified as the central aim which all those involved must work towards. There was a new legislative agenda for service delivery and for the sanctioning of young people who have committed offences. The main legislative changes are summarised in Box 2 and the new pre-court measures and court disposals are summarised in Box 6 in Chapter 5 and in Box 8 in Chapter 6.

There was a dramatic extension of previous multi-agency trends bringing together staff from the police, probation, education and health services to work with the former youth justice workers from social services. Precursors to these youth offending teams already existed in some areas - for example in Northamptonshire and Oxfordshire - and they had focused on dealing with early stage offenders who had not previously been to court. These pre-court diversion panels became fairly widespread in the 1980s and the Northamptonshire model (see NACRO, 1998) was referred to in the Audit Commission's review of youth justice as a model which should be replicated

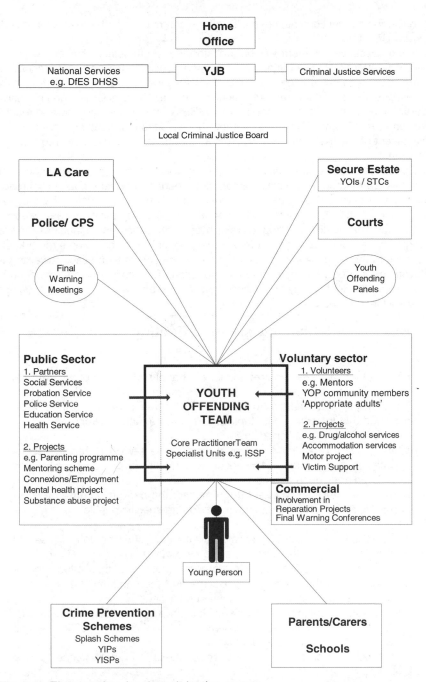

Figure 1: Elements in a local youth justice system

nationally. The connections between the various contributors in the new youth justice are shown in Figure 1.

Another essential element of the transformed youth justice system was the significance attached to evaluation and monitoring. Evaluation was made a condition of early development funding from the Youth Justice Board to set up specialist interventions and to pilot subsequent initiatives such as Referral Orders and Intensive Supervision and Surveillance Programmes (ISSPs). Information systems and routine collection of monitoring data were built into the guidelines for setting up the YOTs. Achievement of key performance indicators subsequently became a pre-requisite for further funding.

Each of these developments was in keeping with the 'new public management' which has permeated the public sector more generally in attempts to increase efficiency and save money. Cost factors were undoubtedly one reason for the 'sea change' in the youth justice system. *Misspent Youth* (Audit Commission, 1996) was the first of several publications calling for reform of youth justice on financial as well as other grounds and the subsequent White Paper and legislation bore some remarkable similarities to the proposals it contained. This orientation of all practice towards the achievement of specified targets and the reduction of recidivism plus the integrated use of information technology to develop evidence-based practice has amounted to a radical shift in 'practice culture'.

Box 2: Post-1998 legislation affecting youth justice

1998 Crime and Disorder Act
- Local authorities were required to carry out audits of the pattern of crime in their areas and were to prioritise crime prevention in their decisions.
- The principle of *doli incapax* for 10-12 year olds was reversed, i.e. it would be assumed that they knew that their actions were seriously wrong unless the reverse could be established.
- Inter-agency youth offending teams were to be set up to replace social services' youth workers and to work to the principal aim of reducing offending by children and young people.
- A Youth Justice Board was set up to monitor the performance of the YOTs according to the administration of the following specific principles:

1. The swift administration of justice so that every young person accused of breaking the law has the matter resolved without delay.
2. Confronting young offenders with the consequences of their offending, for themselves and their family, their victims and the community and helping them to develop a sense of personal responsibility.
3. Intervention which tackles the particular factors (personal, family, social, educational or health) that put the young person at risk of offending and which strengthens 'protective factors'.
4. Punishment proportionate to the seriousness and persistence of the offending.

5. Encouraging reparation to victims by young offenders.
6. Reinforcing the responsibilities of parents.

1998 The Human Rights Act
Came into force October 2000 and incorporates into UK law various rights and freedoms that were set out in the European Convention on Human Rights, to which the UK has been committed since 1951. The main implication is that it is no longer necessary to go to Strasbourg to make a case that rights have been breached by a public authority - for example, Article 6 - Right to a fair trial; Article 7 - No punishment without law; and Article 2 of Protocol 1 - Right to Education.

1999 Youth Justice and Criminal Evidence Act
Part 1 of the Act introduced a new mandatory sentencing disposal - *the referral order* - for 10-17 year olds convicted in court for the first time and pleading guilty. The disposal involves referring young people to a youth offender panel comprising one YOT member and two community members. The work of the panels is to incorporate the underlying principles of restorative justice: making restoration to the victim; achieving reintegration into the community and enabling the offender to take responsibility for the consequences of their behaviour. Part 2 makes provisions for witnesses who find giving evidence in criminal proceedings difficult because they: are children; have a physical or mental disability; are frightened of retaliation or distressed by the nature of the offence. These include:

• Screens to ensure the witness cannot see the accused.
• Giving evidence by live television link.
• Excluding people from the courtroom so that evidence can be given in a more private setting.
• Allowing a video-recorded interview with the witness.
• Allowing as evidence pre-recorded videoed cross-examination.

2000 Powers of Criminal Courts (Sentencing) Act
Designed mainly to consolidate legislation on sentencing and other powers which was previously found in several different statutes. Also includes some provisions about the enforcement of sentences and the treatment of defaulters.

2000 Race Relations (Amendment) Act
Requires public authorities to become proactive in preventing discrimination. The 'Public Duty' provision therefore made racial equality central to all youth justice services and policy decision making.

At the time when we were commencing our in-depth study of the Oxfordshire pathway YOT (see Introduction) the legislation was still relatively fresh and the plans for implementing the new arrangements were still being issued. Pronouncements about what was to come varied depending on their source. Official statements conveyed confidence that the youth crime problem was about to be resolved. In a press release to announce funding for intervention programmes, the then Home Secretary Jack Straw referred to the:

> *...comprehensive programme to crack down on crime and the causes of crime [which] draws a line under the chronic failure of the previous Conservative Government to do anything constructive about the crisis of youth crime*
>
> (Home Office Press Release, 1999)

The policy statement of the Youth Justice Board stated that:

> *The Board will reduce: the seriousness of offending by children and young people; the need to use youth courts; the proportion of young people who acquire a conviction in court; the use of custody for children and young people; inadequate regimes in secure facilities for children and young people.*

Among other declarations of intent, it announced that:

> *The Board will: promote a culture which treats young people fairly and regardless of background in which young people believe they have opportunities to contribute to society and can choose whether or not to offend ...[and] a youth justice system...which works in partnership with services for children and young people and with other partnerships helping to renew communities.*

In contrast to these confident assertions, some academic analysts were forecasting that the reforms would reverse the benefits of previous practice and would amount to youth *in*justice (e.g. see contributions to Goldson, 2000). It was anticipated that the new system would criminalise more children and would result in an increase in the numbers in custody.

Meanwhile, on a local level, practitioners were setting out on this new venture with considerable cheerfulness and optimism. For those working directly with young people, there was the prospect of access to better services. And for those taking hold of the managerial reins it represented an opportunity to sit around a table with chief managers of various agencies to talk about how each would now play a part in tackling youth crime.

CHAPTER 3

Establishing and Managing a Multi-agency Approach

This study of youth offending services took place during the period of, what might generally be described as, early development. As they embarked on the local enterprise of developing joined-up services to tackle youth offending, a member of the strategic management group, appointed to steer the development of the youth offending team, summed up the shared mood of pragmatic optimism:

> One of the most exciting aspects of the Crime and Disorder Act and the new arrangements for youth justice is that they bring together several different agencies who are all essentially looking at the same problem, all eating up public money trying to do something about it but generally bumping into each other all over the place. So I am totally sold on joined-up service if it can be achieved.

> (Police service area manager)

Within the period of early development there were two distinguishable phases: a 'formative stage' when the staff were recruited, resources obtained, services created and developed and partnerships were formed; and a 'consolidation stage' to ensure the continuity of core practice and essential specialist services and to attend to the detail of procedures and service delivery. In this chapter we will focus on issues affecting the strategic management of youth justice services during these two stages of their early development.

Formation of joined-up services

The requirement placed on local authorities to form youth offending teams and to determine youth justice plans presented them with a major challenge. It coincided with a period when all the partner agencies - police, probation, education, health and social services - were experiencing considerable reorganisation in their own right. A stream of government initiatives and funding opportunities had resulted in new activities, services and inter-agency projects. The boundaries of services were being redrawn and it was sometimes unclear precisely which services were joining up with which. This state of flux and fluidity, therefore, was the context in which the youth offending teams were set up. It meant that the period of early development, which is usually a time of 'teething problems' and pressure in normal circumstances, was additionally unsettled and taxing.

On the plus side, helping to offset a potentially chaotic start, some guiding principles could be drawn from the experiences of nine YOTs set up in 1999 to pilot the new arrangements for youth justice. Unfortunately - such was the rapid pace of development and implementation - legislation and policy was decided before there was an opportunity to learn from the final results of the evaluation of the pilot YOTs, but the interim findings, providing examples of good and bad practice in advance of the nationwide establishment of YOTs, were circulated (Holdaway et al., 2001). Also, the Home Office issued a circular with specific advice on how the teams should be formed and managed and on appropriate roles for team members (Home Office, 1999). This initial guidance and regulation was perceived as providing a useful and necessary framework while still leaving scope for local initiative:

> *I think the prescriptive element the Board has come out with has been the right one. It has been helpful. When you compare it to the Connexions Service which hasn't had the same prescriptive push, it is just a complete woolly...and nobody has really got a handle on what it will do. Whereas if you said 'What does a YOT do?' everywhere around the country there would be a lot of similarities, and you could make coherent sense of it...So yes I think it has been helpful.*
>
> (First YOT manager)

As time progressed however, the extent of regulation and instruction from the Board, including amendments to previous directions, increased. There was considerable pressure to put procedures in place at high speed. The pace of development gave rise to concerns that the quality of the work might be compromised.

> *It has been very, very fast and I have only just kept up with it. And the compromise has been the quality and the bedding things in. You know, you've done one thing, you're onto the next and you can't properly get it in. But the Government needed quick wins, that's the way politics runs and I can't see how it could have been done in any other way.*
>
> (First YOT manager)

The first tasks, once the YOT manager had been appointed, were to secure inter-agency partnerships, obtain funding and build up the infrastructure for the YOT. The key players, especially at this early stage, were the newly appointed YOT manager and the chief executive of the county council (who also chaired the strategic management group for the YOT). Important strategies which they adopted in forming the youth justice services were to: build on provision and services already in existence; dovetail the YOT's plans with the plans of partner agencies; gain funding and other contributions from partner agencies on a voluntary rather than mandatory basis. The following account provides examples of how these strategies were applied in getting services set up and launched.

Funding

Home Office and Youth Justice Board guidelines for funding the YOT and its services suggested that one way forward would be for partner agencies to discuss a pooled budget in which each contributed according to a funding formula on a mandatory basis. The chief executive doubted whether such a prescribed model for funding would result in a motivated partnership in which each was committed to the goals. Instead, the tactic was to emphasise the voluntary nature of the partnership and to base negotiations on trust and mutual understanding. Thus, when some of the partners came to the first meeting emphasising their inability to contribute because of funding cuts, they were asked what they could offer instead of cash. This flexibility may have been crucial to gaining co-operation:

> *The ability, in a sense, to move the negotiations between the cash and non-cash was a very important part of enabling and motivating them to play an effective role in the process. If there's a pre-conceived idea that the only way you can become a member of this team is to pay cash and that's the only contribution that's going to be acceptable, then I think the effect of that will be highly detrimental. I think it would have meant that we got off to a very bad start and everyone would have been very annoyed. There would have been less commitment, less participation from some of the services.*
>
> (Chief executive)

Services that were initially making minimal contributions were, through this flexible approach, enabled to come into the process. The chief executive suggested that there might have been an element of tacit peer group pressure because a non-contributing agency would be aware of the input of other agencies and would eventually decide it 'can't go on just doing the washing up in order to stay in'. Other negotiating principles were used in order to win the trust of partner agencies. For example, the main funding partner was promised that the county council would match whatever funding they put into the pot.

Joined-up planning for the provision of youth justice services

Gaining the co-operation of other agencies was achieved partly via the discussions of the multi-agency strategy group but was largely the accomplishment of a skilled YOT manager. The following extract from an interview with one of the strategy group members provides a good indication of how the YOT manager tackled this task and the degree of success:

> *She has been broadly successful in setting the YOT up as a structure which improves our mainstream services, and which is not simply something else to co-ordinate. So we do think of it as our YOT; it's not just something which is a bolt-on extra over there. I think that what (the YOT Manager) has tried to avoid is setting up something that is just not linked in with what we are trying to do generally. On everything that she is wanting to develop she has come and said how does this fit with what you are trying to do? How can we enhance what we are trying to do, rather than set up something which is parallel with what we are trying to do which could actually make the situation more complex or whatever? And I think that approach was a real strength.*
>
> (Member of the strategy group)

This approach exemplifies the suggestion by Liddle and Gelsthorpe (1994: 4) that the aims of multi-agency projects should be 'sold by key organisers through the grid of each agency's own priorities, purposes and practices'. A clear example of where this occurred was in connections made between the Youth Justice Plan and the Education Development Plan. A partnership with the YOT made sense to the Education Service because joint work to reduce school exclusion and raise educational achievement was clearly relevant to its own agenda while at the same time tackling one of the risk factors associated with offending.

The carrot of external funding for setting up joint projects was obviously another factor which helped to win over partner agencies. However, despite such incentives and regardless of the effectiveness or otherwise of the manager's powers of persuasion, there were inevitable limits to what agencies felt able to contribute because of their own internal considerations. The strategy group members spoke of the strong sense of co-operation and goodwill but also a tension they experienced when sitting round the table between representing their own organisation and developing the YOT's agenda. Public services generally were having to cope with ever-increasing demands to deliver more and improve their performance and to reduce their expenditure. Regardless of how much they were committed to the reforms of youth justice, the needs of their own organisation and those of the YOT presented them with a dilemma. The requirement to second staff to join the youth offending team was particularly difficult for some services. Short of staff themselves, they were understandably reluctant to sacrifice their best staff. A manager from the probation service, faced with decisions about seconding staff to the YOT, provided insight into how onerous such conflicts of interest can be:

> *I argued that we needed to be very careful about meeting other people's agendas rather than our own. It was at a time when we were running out of experienced qualified probation officers and our reputation could be seriously at risk...it's not a resistance to getting involved...I believe [the youth justice reforms] are probably the only way you are going to get the right mix of skills and experiences and break-up the youth justice culture, and get alternatives to custody and diversion. It is important that we demonstrate our commitment publicly. We were one of the first services to do so...We had two officers who applied to be seconded. Two very good officers. We'd weep about losing either of them. There is a sense of loss...I'm protective of my own organisation, but I believe passionately that - when I'm at the YOT meeting - that we've got to get this right.*

(Manager from probation service)

Choosing in favour of the YOT also meant placing confidence in new, untried services, and this felt risky. The partner agencies hoped that the results of monitoring and evaluation would provide quick confirmation that their investment had not been misplaced. Establishing a link with each partner agency's agenda was ambitious and not always achieved. This was particularly so for agencies that have not traditionally seen themselves as concerned with crime. The health service officials sitting on the strategy group were the least easily convinced that there would be mutual benefits from the partnership. Indeed the health service was the only one which conveyed any of the 'sense of compulsion' and 'shotgun weddings' which Bailey and Williams (2000: 5) described as accompanying the formation of youth offending services. In trying to integrate youth justice with health services the deceptive simplicity of the joined-up service ideal was made especially apparent. The health service managers were facing new agendas of their own, which had been centrally imposed, and which they were having to deal with as a matter of urgency. The Chief Executive conveyed the need for local ambitions to be cognisant of these realities:

> *It is alright for those on the strategic summit to look down and argue that of course health is a dimension to criminal behaviour...and at a sort of strategic level is a perfectly rational way of looking at it. The difficulty comes when you are actually putting themes together and you say 'What do we mean by that? How do we translate a very simple model into a daily practical reality of being with this child or with that child?' Also you have to live in the real world that those institutions, be they primary care groups, general practitioners, hospitals, are actually having a set of agendas imposed on them from a whole range of silos where this particular issue is actually quite a long way down the hierarchy. So if you ask the question, notwithstanding there's a legal duty on the Health Service to participate in it, if you ask the question "What is going to get the Chief Executive of the Health Authority fired? What is he afraid of losing his job for?' it is not implementing the Crime and Disorder or the youth offending strategy or anything like that. It is making sure that the waiting list problem is sorted out in his area of responsibility...It comes down to this basic problem about how we try and run public services with excessive silo instructions.*

(Chief executive)

From the perspectives of the health service, the YOT's agenda was experienced as a 'bolt-on' extra and a 'top-down national initiative, not a bottom-up initiative. One health official compared it to the telephone service, *NHS Direct*: a good idea but one for which there is no local ownership and which is additional to important local priorities. OYOT focused on building up a dedicated mental health service as part of the YOT but met with some resistance from the Child and Adolescent Mental Health Service (CAMHS) (see Chapter 6). Some tension was perhaps inevitable because the local CAMHS was at that time focused towards the specialist end rather than a community-based end.

The difficulty in engaging the health sector was matched by the experience of other YOTs around the country. Similarly, the report on the Crime and Disorder Reduction Partnerships found the health sector to have been a reluctant partner because of lack of resources but also because health representatives have 'fundamental doubts about the role of the health authority in crime and disorder activities' (Phillips et al., 2002: 10).

A shared infrastructure

Some youth offending teams were able to build on previous multi-agency arrangements. OYOT was a case in point: a fast start was facilitated by the prior inroads made by the Crime Intervention Service which had provided projects at the pre-court stage and was aimed at diverting children and young people from the criminal justice system. Indeed, the YOT took over some of the projects of the former Crime Intervention Service plus many of its staff. This take-over provided a significant head start for meeting the requirements of the new legislation and was partly the reason why it gained 'pathway' status.

Nevertheless, the infrastructure for the youth offending team had to be built up from next to nothing. The manager emphasised from the start that the YOT would not be, and should not be, a self-sufficient organisation. Instead, decisions were made about what the YOT needed for itself and what it could more efficiently draw from the county council or partner agencies. It took time, and trial and error, to settle on where the lines should be drawn. While the services of the county council could be utilised to a certain extent, there was still a need for basic administrative systems and procedures to be met in-house. Personnel services were partly in-house and partly a matter for other agencies in the case of staff seconded to the YOT by them, but oversight of personnel matters was secured from the chief executive's department. The YOT processed all its own invoices and carried out recruitment and selection, but called upon the treasurers' department for oversight and shared accountability. The chief executive's department remained accountable for the financial side in liaison with the YOT manager and administrator.

There were no clear health and safety procedures during the early months and the deficits became increasingly clear. Following an incident in one of the buildings used by YOT staff, health and safety officers from both the police and from social services were called in with resulting confusion. The two representatives, following different protocols and union guidelines, disagreed about what were acceptable working conditions for staff. It was decided, therefore, that health and safety inspections should be provided by a single agency to be carried out on a regular basis. Health and safety services were eventually secured, as an in-service contribution, from a third partner agency. This was a good example of how the YOT linked up with the infra structure of other services.

In the dynamic fast-changing early months the YOT did not have much of an infra structure and it quickly outgrew its staff capacity. Administrative staff had been in short supply and basic procedures like processing invoices were not established. The YOT manager often picked up the office telephone. A year on, once more staff had been recruited, services developed and the infra structure secured, the manager was able to reflect that the YOT had become recognised as a credible organisation in its own right - though not a *self-contained* organisation, because it relied upon control mechanisms bought in from other agencies.

The 'formative' stage began with buoyancy and optimism under its dynamic leadership and at a time when the largesse of the Youth Justice Board was attracting the interest of partner agencies. The first months were an exciting period of growth which inspired staff and fitted well with the Youth Justice Board's consistently positive publicity about the reforms it was overseeing. The first manager was adept in promoting the YOT, making it visible to the media and thereby attracting large numbers of volunteers to participate in the service plus keeping it within the sights of the YJB. During this period much of the focus had been on bringing disciplines, services and community together and in setting up a wide range of services, policies and protocols. As one of the strategy group put it: 'We have assembled the chess pieces on the table. And now the game can begin'. Reaching this milestone was a substantial and exhausting process.

Consolidation

Reviewing the first 18 months of whirlwind development, the YOT manager and other staff were increasingly pointing to a need for consolidation and 'bedding down' of whatever has been put in place. Operational managers were recognising that what had been accomplished so far should be audited and improved, with corresponding protocols drawn up. They were aware the quality of the work being done would be improved by clarification and confirmation of procedures and greater attention to detail to ensure that national standards would be met. The metaphor of 'surface gloss' was used more than once by the manager and other staff to refer to yearnings for opportunities to bed down and consolidate services put in place and ensure that they were more than superficially impressive. The appointment of a deputy manager (an additional post, reflecting the expansion of the YOT) and a change in the top manager position approximately coincided with the move from the formative stage to that of consolidation.

For the second manager of the YOT, there was little ambiguity in seeing the YOT as a separate, free-standing agency providing it had sufficient command over a pooled budget and could make decisions about how the money should be spent without needing to consult partner agencies on every occasion. It was important, though, to have some of its own staff rather than simply being a referee between seconded staff and their parent agencies; and it was crucial that the budget should be adequate.

This 'pathway' YOT had attracted considerable 'pump-priming' money from the YJB and so the second manager coming into office was surprised to discover that the initial pooled budget had been 'just about enough to keep people in paper clips' and that the future budget was uncertain. Most of the development funding had been dedicated to the development of specialised projects and tapered over a three year period to encourage increasing contributions from elsewhere and eventual financial in-dependence from the YJB. After the first few months of operation the YOT was successful in bidding to pilot referral orders and ISSPs. The investment of activity and funding in these two, very substantial, enterprises further distracted from the inadequacy of basic provision. National comparative data revealed that the con-tributions from partner agencies had been comparatively low. On some levels, a 'Rolls Royce' service was being established, but there were insufficient resources for 'core services': assessment and preparation of pre-sentence reports, court duties; one-to-one supervision of young people; case-records. The first YOT manager commented that:

> YJB grants are being continually thrown out to us still. At the moment there is one for literacy and numeracy, one for mentoring, there is another appropriate adult one coming, one for mentoring…It is just madness the amount of set-up stuff that is still coming.

Looking back over the first 12 months, a member of staff described this formative period as one of 'champagne and caviar but not enough bread'. These successive bidding opportunities seemed to augur well for the future, giving an illusory sense that either the YJB or partner services would make continual contributions. However, the funding arrangements had encouraged a short-term approach of 'get it while you can' rather than future attention to 'exit strategies' for funding the specialised projects once development funding ceased. The second YOT manager concluded that the initial largesse of the YJB had been unhelpful because it had distracted partner agencies from their collective longer-term responsibilities for strategic planning and funding of arrangements to tackle youth crime.

The YOT started out during the formative stage with the advantage of a strategy group chaired by the chief executive of the county council and composed of top-tier managers from the partner agencies. Advice given by some members - particularly in between meetings - to the first manager was 'invaluable'. However the group meetings gradually became less strategic in function to the point where the manager felt the main purpose was simply to keep members up to date with developments. By then a new chief executive in the county council had withdrawn from chairing the strategy group because of the impracticality of maintaining a presence at *all* such joined-up initiatives. The second manager observed that the group had been focused on steering the YOT rather than on involving their own services in strategies for addressing youth crime, as had been intended by the legislation. He therefore endeavoured to restate the intended terms of reference as specified by the Home Office and the YJB, and involved the strategy group members in systematically going through the performance measures to consider what implications each had for their own service.

Steps were taken to rescue the YOT from its, then, hazardous funding situation. First, it needed its own budget, with separate allocations for staffing, training, accommodation and so forth. Previously there had not been a YOT budget as such, because the development funding had been earmarked for distinct projects rather than to the YOT as a whole. Also there had been insufficient business planning, again because of the short-term nature of the funding. The services of the county council treasurers had been used but in managing the YOT's accounts and salaries they had not been operating as normal because of the unusual nature of the funding arrangements. The deputy YOT manager carried out a zero-based budget exercise in order to calculate unit costs of activity and build these into the picture of what the YOT should be spending, as opposed to what it had been spending. The YJB had not (at the time of writing) provided a model of what the appropriate amount of funding should be for each activity but a business plan was formulated, based on unit costing, to clarify future expenditure.

Another surprise emerged from the issuing by the YJB of comparative tables of YOT funding per head, which took into account both YJB funding and the contributions of partner agencies. This supposedly well-funded 'pathway' YOT was, in fact, in the bottom third of the table for funding per head. Funding from partner agencies, which had seemed generous at the time, proved to be well below the average funding received by other YOTs. The arising budget deficits were met by additional funding from the county council, with plans that this would be reduced in future years but that partner agencies would increase their contributions.

The funding opportunities provided by the YJB had concentrated attention on the specialist projects more than on the central work of the YOT done by practitioners - court services, reports, supervision - and their needs for resources, training, support systems and suitable accommodation for working with young people. After the first 18 months all major specialist resources had either been acquired or arranged. The second YOT manager's view, therefore, was that it would be inappropriate to take up further bidding opportunities unless they were clearly 'strategically sensible' opportunities, 'because we can learn the lessons that sometimes they can get in the way of what is actually our core business'. On the other hand, the YOT had been struggling to deliver a high volume of core services on a relatively low budget and with a relatively low number of practitioners. The number of staff had increased but the recent intake had included unqualified staff who needed additional support and training. Operational procedures also needed attention. The strategic approach adopted by the head of youth services, therefore, was to 'take the next year as an opportunity to address what we need to meet our core business and ensure it is of sufficient quality'. Echoing similar sentiments, a senior practitioner reflected: 'We have the gloss and it looks good...Now let's concentrate on developing the quality'. Although the excitement and dynamism of the early stages had been replaced by a quieter, less dramatic period in the YOT's life, this was a welcome opportunity for the new services to be embedded and improved.

Other factors in the development of a joined-up service

Across the formative and consolidation stages, matters of leadership and of partnership coterminosity were of continuing relevance.

The leadership factor

Various investigators have found that a critical factor in the success of partnership initiatives is having a strong leader. For example, in their evaluation of the Crime Reduction Programme, Hedderman and Williams (2001) found that the leadership of the project manager 'seems to be *the* factor which determines whether implementation is successful'. They identified the qualities of imagination, stamina, networking, management skills and dogged determination as relevant to success. This being the case, the selection committee for our pathway YOT deserves credit for choosing the right manager to *establish* the YOT. Other leadership qualities are also of importance for later stages of development.

In addition to the qualities listed above, the first YOT manager brought a conviction that 'partnership working is the right approach' and a keenness to develop a youth service which would be publicly accountable as well as accountable to partner agencies and central government. Bolstered by this commitment, she took up the challenge of 'starting from scratch'. Initially there were no resources other than herself 'running around, doing everything without a base'. As the YOT was launched and set about doing its business, quickly increasing in scope and size, the single-handed strategic and overall operational management called for large reserves of stamina and a grasp of every aspect of the YOT's services. In addition to 'endless report-writing, paper-churning and wheeling out' the first manager, partly from necessity, had what other staff called a 'hands-on approach' to the daily problems which arose for staff in their practice. It was unsurprising therefore, after the formative stage, when the strategy group agreed to the appointment of a deputy manager who would focus on operational delivery.

Leadership also has a relational dimension and this is particularly important in an inter-agency setting. Faulkner (2001) has argued that to achieve successful partnership arrangements it is necessary to go beyond mere mechanics to values and the relationships between individuals. The first manager of the YOT, a charismatic leader and an excellent networker, was successful in securing those necessary inter-professional relationships and in promoting the YOT as a credible and recognised public service. When the first YOT manager left the position, there was a real danger that inter-agency relations would be a casualty. Fortunately, the successive manager came into the post with a ready-made, extensive network of local relationships established during previous posts.

The original manager described her main strengths as 'being able to see how to set things up and also the steps needed to be able to go and do it'. She identified that 'stamina and tenacity was in there somewhere because you just couldn't give up'. Partners saw her as 'someone with an enormous amount of energy and a can-do attitude'. Such qualities gave prospective partners a sense of confidence that their own investment would reap dividends. Having met the challenge of setting it up she questioned whether she would be as 'good at maintaining and digging it in'. This was never put to the test. The next major task of ensuring that the newly formed edifice would not collapse was one which was taken up by someone else.

When one manager takes over from another comparisons are always made. Which manager was better at this and worse at that is less relevant to the lessons to be drawn from our case-study than what was highlighted by the change. Leadership qualities are diverse and the most appropriate leader to sustain a project may not be the best to get it off the ground, and vice versa. Initially, some staff expressed disappointment that a second creative and visionary YOT manager had not been filched from another YOT, but this was quickly followed by assurances that perhaps there could now be a respite from the constant development and change and a much needed period of consolidation. The new manager came from a managerial post in the local social services and brought a reputation for being a realistic consolidator - arguably just what this YOT needed after its flyaway start. In addition to the skills and qualities brought to bear, the professional background of managers is part of what they bring into the management post. The first manager had an appropriate background in the probation service, by then sensitised to evidence-based practice. The second manager brought years of experience in the county's social services division, controlling a budget and was sitting on numerous inter-agency committees. As he explained:

The other thing is where you are coming from. The benefit that I bring to the YOT from having been in this county in the role that I had for a long period of time is that I slot into a lot of the multi-agency structures, just because I was there already. And also I already know [the other managers] so I can actually choose how to play with them. So it is very different for me. And also having to do some of the other things as well. Apart from control of a budget, I have had a singularly different management experience than [the first manager] had.

All of this has facilitated continuity and made it possible to slip into many strategic multi-agency roles and to expand the YOT's local network 'at a stroke'. The management role taken on by the second YOT manager was very different from the corresponding role of the first YOT manager which had been both strategic and operational. By the time the second manager took over the post there was 'a very able deputy, operationally managing the majority of the service, including managing the operational managers'. The title of the 'YOT Manager' changed to 'Head of Youth Services' to reflect the fact that it had become, more purely, a strategic job

The trouble with boundaries

A frequent observation made by chief officers taking part in this joined-up venture was the sheer practical difficulty in making it work when the geographic boundaries of services, and their respective networks, are not coterminous. Managers wished that national policy makers in departments of state (the Department of Environment being an exception) would understand the significance of aligning boundaries. Some counties and some YOTs were affected by this problem more than others, given the variability in their size and areas covered. OYOT was at least able to link up with other countywide services, but it might have been more logical to have a Thames Valley youth service to be aligned with Thames Valley police service and strategic health authority.

The chief executive gave a graphic account of how misalignment translates into logistical problems, which it is helpful to reproduce here:

If it is the case that if you have misaligned boundaries then it doesn't matter how important everybody thinks partnership working is, it actually gets much more complicated - almost exponentially more complicated, the more units you have. It's a bit like, you know any sort of human structure. You and I can relate on a one to one basis. When we add a third person to our team it isn't a third more difficult to maintain the liaison, it's double the difficulty to maintain the liaison. And as you build up, the problems increase exponentially rather than simply numerically. And I think the same problem arises with partnerships. For example, it wouldn't surprise me if there were serious problems in Berkshire where the unitary authorities that they created down there are too small to have their own youth offending team and therefore they've had to coalesce for the youth offending team. Well that immediately brings all sorts of problems because you have two education departments and two social services departments - and once you start doing that you cause all sorts of difficulties about joint working. And conversely, of course, the other way, if you have a very large area...where you then sub-divide. You know, you have an area of jurisdiction which is too big for a youth offending team so you start sub-dividing it. Well, at that point, if you've created a jurisdiction which is too big and has several YOTs in one area, why should one then expect the chief executive to chair all of them? In a sense there are problems which come from the discontinuity of different boundaries. I only wish that civil servants in the Department of Health, civil servants in the Home Office, civil servants in the Youth Justice Board would understand that partnership working is made much more complicated and much more complex by differential boundaries.

Managers in the area which we investigated felt they were better off than corresponding teams in other regions because quite a few pieces of the complex jigsaw puzzle did fit together reasonably well. Even so, there were some disparities. For example, negotiations with the health service became more difficult when the health service economy changed and was reorganised into primary care trusts (PCTs). This meant that the chief officer attending was only representing one of the PCTs rather that the whole of the county and had no budgetary control over the other PCTs. Negotiations with the probation service were complicated by the merger between probation services across different counties (the Oxfordshire and Buckinghamshire Probation service - which later merged also with Berkshire, becoming The Thames Valley Probation Service). The local probation service therefore had responsibilities to several lots of youth offending services. The manager of OYOT criticised such mergers as public sector cost-shunting exercises:

It is meant to be more cost-efficient for the overheads of the probation service. What it does is actually shunt the costs of working a partnership to other agencies. So we all start shunting these costs around and in the end somebody - it's like a pass the parcel thing - somebody ends up holding the parcel with the extra costs. The purpose of the exercise is to make sure it's not your responsibility. But the public sector isn't actually being served by this in a sense and I think we would be better off actually trying to rationalise the boundaries.

These struggles with boundaries indicated that the lack of coterminosity between some services was an obstacle to establishing effective joined-up youth services.

Accountability for youth justice services

One of the anomalies that arose from the development of the YOT and its partnerships was a lack of clear lines of accountability. The re-organisation and introduction of new services had dislocated previous management and political arrangements. The YOT manager reported to a strategy group and had helpful meetings on a regular basis with the director of social services, but had no obvious line manager. Six months into the post, the second YOT manager remarked that 'at no point since starting here have I ever had to go to anyone else for anything, for any decision or for anything actually'. Whereas previously, as a manager in social services, he been accountable to councillors, since joining the YOT it had not even been necessary to have the youth justice plan approved by councillors.

Despite this odd lapse in local accountability, the first YOT manager exercised a sense of accountability in a different way, by being open and accessible to the local media, and by emphasising that staff should be able to account for their time and their decisions:

> *I like to think that one of the real achievements is we've set up a service that is accountable to the public...I feel we've made ourselves very accessible and open to the press. And through arrangements for referral orders we've set ourselves up for scrutiny to volunteers that come and work for us, warts and all. We are not trying to hide anything or say we are perfect. That has been quite a hard thing to manage from my point of view. There have been a lot of complaints and concerns. You know: 'It is outrageous that this child is not at school' and 'Did you know that yet again one of your staff didn't turn up?' all that sort of stuff. But I think that should make staff work in an accountable way. As professionals, we can't just assume that we do what we want. And I think that for me is probably the thing that I will take away the most. I feel I've set up something that could be up for scrutiny from the public. The community members who work with us on referral orders are only a small section of the public, so we could do more - but that is my philosophical approach.*

(First YOT manager)

On a central rather than local level each YOT manager and local authority was under definite national directions to set up youth justice services and develop a plan. YOTs were made accountable to the Youth Justice Board and required to produce quarterly statistics and to meet performance targets. While the YJB has been responsible for monitoring YOTs, they have not been subject to independent scrutiny since their inauguration in 2000. Not before time, a programme for the inspection of YOTs began in April 2003. The inspections are led by HM Inspectorate of Probation but are being carried out by a consortium of inspectorates (probation, police, prisons, social services, and education) in consultation with the Home Office and the YJB. The aim is to inspect all 154 YOTs over a five to six year cycle.

CHAPTER 4

The Inter-agency Team and its New Practice Culture

At the heart of each local youth justice system is the youth offending team - neither a gang of young offenders as the name might suggest to the uninitiated, nor a type of sailing vessel as is conveyed by the sound of its neologised abbreviation YOT, but - a co-operative of practitioners drawn from several public services whose mandate brings them into contact with young people at risk of (re)offending. The professionals who had most responsibility for young offenders prior to the Crime and Disorder Act 1998 - youth justice workers and some probation officers - have been joined by representatives from the police service, education and the health service. Some YOTs have additional team members drawn from the voluntary sector, such as drugs workers.

It was made clear in the White Paper *No More Excuses* and other government discussion papers that the YOTs could not simply be the former youth justice teams under a new name, but that there was to be a radical overhaul of working practices and change of goal and emphasis:

> *In the past, the youth justice system has suffered from changing policy priorities and a lack of consistent direction. The Government believes that there has been confusion about the purpose of the youth justice system and the principles that should govern the way in which young people are dealt with by youth justice agencies. Concerns about the welfare of the young person have too often been seen as in conflict with the aims of protecting the public, punishing offences and preventing offending. This confusion creates real practical difficulties for practitioners and has contributed to the loss of public confidence in the youth justice system. Accordingly, the Crime and Disorder Bill will make clear that the aim of the youth justice system is to prevent offending by young people. The Bill will place a duty on all people working in the youth justice system to have regard to that aim.*

> (Home Office, 1997)

As identified by researchers who evaluated the pilot YOTs 'the challenge [was] nothing less than the development of new ways of working' (Holdaway et al., 2001: 8). This re-organisation was a manifestation of the trend in criminal justice away from penal welfarism to the justice model; away from social work and individualised support to risk management and public protection (Garland, 2001).

While critics saw the 'new youth justice' as a decided move towards a more punitive approach (for example see the volume edited by Goldson, 2000), the mood of practitioners through the first two to three years was, generally, much more sanguine. Indeed, when the YOT first went into operation there was a palpable atmosphere of enthusiastic optimism. Some staff mentioned misgivings that the legislative changes could result in 'net-widening' (bringing more young people into the criminal justice system) or voiced quiet concerns about the adoption of case-management approaches, but the overwhelming mood was one of optimism. They looked forward to inter-agency working (see Box 3), to operating within a wider framework of disposals and sentences, and to an extended range of opportunities for helping young people deal with problems related to offending. As one practitioner put it: 'What we are doing here is not building an empire but trying to access and create the best resources possible for the young people that we work with'.

While the reforms were welcomed as opposed to resisted, as was the case in some of the pilot YOTs (set up a year earlier than other YOTs - see Holdaway et al., 2001), some staff questioned whether there was much that was truly 'new'. The majority of the practitioners forming the YOT had been involved in some capacity in the multi-agency diversion scheme which had been the forerunner of the YOT (known as the Crime Intervention Service). They had previously established projects, such as a parenting and a mentoring project; had already applied restorative justice approaches including work with victims, and already had a pattern of multi-agency networks. There were sufficient continuities with previous developments for them to question what all the fuss was about. Thus they questioned the extent to which there was innovation.

However, the new legislation, additional projects, changed working practices and the sheer pace of development gave a sense of being deluged by change. One unit manager explained:

It has been ever-evolving. There has never been a set menu of what we are doing and what is expected of us. As soon as we were getting up to speed with one aspect of practice, along came another innovation or initiative.

Increasingly, staff did acknowledge that some form of revolution had taken place amounting to a new practice culture. The key changes were that:

- The core youth justice staff were required to work alongside people from different professional backgrounds.
- There was a shift in professional ethos away from welfare to prevention of re-offending.
- It required a shift to evidence-based practice, involving changes in operational practices.

Progress in shifting to evidence-based practice was impeded by chronic delays in the introduction of the electronic data entry and monitoring system. Also, former youth justice staff, who were used to carrying out assessments, resented the length of time required to complete Asset, the systematic assessment tool that had been introduced for use in all YOTs. The terms 'what works', 'effective practice' and 'evidence-based practice' were bandied about without them being necessarily understood by busy practitioners who were facing an influx of new cases. There was a period when the YOT was accommodating extra initiatives and its projects were flourishing, but core practice was barely keeping up. The numbers of young people receiving final warnings and referral orders were greater than had been anticipated. It became apparent, as mentioned previously, that staffing levels for core practice were inadequate, and this was confirmed by comparisons of staffing levels in other YOTs. Staff felt 'too stretched to do a good job' and were not able to meet national standards for frequency of contact and target intervals. At the same time, middle managers had been pulled away from operational concerns by their additional developmental roles. As a result, basic operational systems and the needs of practitioners in coping with new legislation and initiatives were neglected. Added to this, as experienced in other YOTs, there was an 'atmosphere of impermanence' (Bailey and Williams, 2000: 37) resulting from the short-term nature of secondments and either temporary or unsatisfactory office accommodation. Indeed, staff joked that YOT stood for 'you're only temporary'. For one unit, there was also the significant practical problem of carrying out a peripatetic job from a base that was miles away from parking space. None of this was an ideal background for reforming the old practice culture.

Box 3: Comparison between multi-agency and inter-agency services

The terms 'multi-agency' and 'inter-agency' are often used interchangeably. They were helpfully distinguished by Crawford (1997: 119) as follows:

multi-agency services
Various agencies come together to address a problem

inter-agency services
Involves some degree of fusion and melding of relations between agencies

Youth offending services as a whole and the youth justice plan within a jurisdiction exemplify 'multi-agency' provision of services. The practitioner teams that make up a YOT, generally based in the same building and often carrying out the same tasks and functions, are an example par excellence of 'inter-agency' working.

Working together

The creation of youth offending teams was described by Bailey and Williams as rather like 'shotgun weddings between agencies' (2000: 5). They also observed that there were occasional 'turf wars' (2000: 73) between professionals from different backgrounds. This was not the experience in Oxfordshire where there were cordial relations within offices from the start and a very open attitude to the prospect of learning from each other. Interestingly, any opposition or rivalry that did occur tended to be between units serving different areas of the county rather than between professional disciplines. Working together in a team was mainly identified as a positive experience which brought distinct advantages as well as some challenges. In summary, the immediate gains were:

- reciprocal exchange of knowledge
- direct or quicker access to other services and expertise
- improved referral processes

Each of these was seen as helping them to achieve the ideal of a 'seamless service' without the usual delays and communication blocks caused by bureaucratic boundaries. There were some disappointments about delays and continuing gaps in resources (see Chapter 6 for an account of the partnership projects). However, the practitioners generally extolled the virtues of inter-agency working and gave examples of how it had facilitated a holistic approach in which each of the psychosocial and environmental factors related to an individual's offending could be simultaneously addressed (see Burnett and Appleton, 2004).

Specialisms

During the formative months staff debated how best to combine their skills in order to maximise the inter-agency benefits, and the metaphor of 'fruit cake versus fruit salad' was used to speculate on possible outcomes (Hancock, 2000; Burnett and Appleton, 2004). If they all learned and applied the same skills this would allow most of the tasks to be undertaken by whoever was available but, like the ingredients that make up a fruit cake in contrast to fruit salad, it would then be more difficult for them to retain their identifiable specialisms. It had been difficult to cope with the volume of work coming through and would have been helpful to have specialists who were also able to carry out core tasks, such as making assessments and carrying out court duty. On the other hand, it was vital that some staff with specialist experience were available; for example, only the police were able to contact victims, and diagnosing mental health problems required expertise. Over the period of the YOT's development, however, team members' separate professional identities became less distinguishable and the unified identity of 'YOT practitioner' emerged, graphically described by one practitioner as 'this meltdown kind of thing where we are from other agencies but the edges are very fuzzy'. Whereas initially there had been concern about ideas and values being subjugated to a dominant culture brought by youth justice workers, a year into operation there was a sense of cross-disciplinary influence and shared identity.

However, numerically there was a greater presence of youth justice workers in the team than of staff from any of the other professional disciplines. The youth justice workers were more experienced in the essential everyday work and so others depended on them to pass on skills. The shared YOT practitioner identity was therefore inevitably more strongly influenced by them, and when later, the team was joined by a significant number of unqualified support staff who entered without any particular affiliation, they were more likely to be absorbed into this dominant culture. Nevertheless, there is no doubt that the other professionals had been influential. The probation service was ahead in moving to the new culture of risk management and evidence-based practice and so seconded probation staff brought some relevant prior experience. The police members brought a direct 'let's get on with it' attitude. Health and education brought specialist insights which altered practitioners' everyday perspectives.

Skills, training and competencies

The YOTs were formed at a time when house prices were rising steeply in many parts of the country and when the social standing of public service workers had been diminished. Salary levels for at least three of the agencies who contribute to youth justice offered little recompense. Small wonder therefore that youth offending teams have experienced recruitment problems. To help meet the shortfall in staff numbers OYOT introduced the new post of 'YOT Support Worker'. The creation of this job title enabled the recruitment of enthusiastic people with potential, though unqualified and without direct experience of the work. The plan was to use them in a more flexible way, recognising that they were unsuitable for some of the more skilled work. This was met with mixed reactions by existing staff, some of whom were still struggling themselves with unfamiliar tasks they had taken over. Established staff joked that anyone who came to the YOT for a cup of tea and showed an interest became eligible to join the team.

These appointments were seen by some as contributing to a general 'dumbing down' of the work and the skills it required. Earlier, a YJB training course had already led to such an impression. The same, compulsory, six day training course had been provided for all practitioners in the youth justice system, and more experienced staff felt that - apart from a useful opportunity to network with other staff - it had been a waste of their time because it taught them little and had been 'aimed at the lowest common denominator'. The recruitment of staff without work experience in youth justice initially placed a burden on qualified staff who were required to pass on their skills and train the recruits. The YOT manager explained that the objective was to take advantage of people's interest in being involved and diverse experience but 'without trying to kid ourselves that they are going to be able to do the same job that YOT staff are doing'. It was admitted though by operational managers that staff shortage meant that occasionally cases were allocated to staff who were not experienced enough to hold them. To be fair to the policy of recruiting support staff and to the abilities of those appointed, in-service training was subsequently provided for them and experienced staff were pleased with their progress and contribution.

New ways of working

Two labels often used to describe the way in which practice in youth justice has shifted are 'evidence-based practice' and 'case-management'. Though different in meaning, there is an overlap between these two concepts in their practical implementation. Both involve the use of systematic procedures for monitoring, collecting and using information and both make use of information technology. 'Evidence-based practice' requires a use of interventions that have been shown by research evidence to be the most effective and the introduction of procedures that will support the accumulation of such evidence. There are various definitions and models of 'case-management' (Holt, 2000) but what it means in practical terms within a youth justice context is a shift in the focus of practice from direct work with young people to management of the work which is carried out with them. These developments represent a switch in practice from individualised one-to-one supervision, based largely on the discretion of the supervising practitioner, to the use of systematic assessment procedures and referral to specialists and programmes, informed by research into effective practice. This practice transition has resulted in a job which is more desk-bound and mechanistic, involving more contact with colleagues and less contact with the young people and their families.

Reactions to the changes were mixed. While most staff welcomed the opportunity to use computers - especially if they had had prior experience in using them - other practice developments gave rise to apprehensions. Former youth justice workers, not surprisingly, were the most defensive of former practice. First, they were concerned that preoccupations with data collection, monitoring and evaluation would increasingly distance them from what they saw as their main skill and potential to be effective: direct work with young people (sometimes referred to as 'casework') and from the direct youth work they had chosen to do in entering the service, and which they regarded as the most valuable and meaningful aspect of their job. Secondly, they had suspicions that such tasks, rather then benefiting their own practice, might be used as fodder to serve political ends in promoting a more punitive approach.

Evidence-based practice and technology

Evidence-based practice, sometimes referred to as 'effective practice' and 'what works', is practice that is informed by evaluation and research to establish which interventions are the most effective in reducing re-offending. The accumulation and use of such findings necessitates the routine use of systematic assessment, monitoring and evaluation, supported by electronic information systems. Such an overhaul in day to day operations, plus appreciation of what is involved and its implications, do not happen overnight. The evaluators of the pilot YOTs advised that evidence-based practice would be central and would require relevant training in order to 'create and sustain a culture of work suited to the objectives of the Crime and Disorder Act' (Holdaway et al., 2001: 8). The six days of training provided by the YJB were very broad-based and did not include in-depth preparation for such a culture change. It was not clear that what was meant and intended by 'evidence-based practice' was well articulated, including its links to assessment procedures, to the 'what works agenda' and to information technology. One member of staff commented that: 'There is token mention of it, but there is an awful lot of emphasis on Asset [the assessment tool]'.

Electronic information systems

The adoption of such a practice culture within Oxfordshire YOT was slow and faltering. Various factors got in the way, including being short-staffed, the stream of directions, instructions and developments coming from the YJB and government and - not least - the operation of the electronic information system. Adopting and using an electronic information system was one of the most radical elements of the change in practice culture, requiring new skills and a different perspective on the purpose of data collection and recording. OYOT arranged for the installation of the Youth Offending Information System (YOIS) and appropriate training in its use. An information officer, who was appointed to analyse the data collected and to present statistical information for performance monitoring, helped staff to adjust to using computers for data entry and case-management systems. Staff were not surprised by the protracted installation period and technical hitches, given that computerised systems are notorious for such problems. The technical problems continued though after the system was in operation. There were chronic setbacks because of incompatibilities with the county council systems and because the system kept crashing. Staff then became increasingly reluctant to regard this development as one which would increase the effectiveness of practice. Rather it was seen as an obstruction to getting the work done.

Assessment procedures

Assessment is a necessary element of evidence-based practice in criminal justice, and the case-management approach. The YJB commissioned the development of a purpose-designed assessment tool, known as Asset. Perhaps to signal its importance to practitioners in the youth justice system, until recently the name always appeared in capitals in Youth Justice Board publications even though Asset was not an acronym. This tool facilitates systematic assessment of the circumstances and characteristics of young people who have offended, scoring each factor according to its degree of association with their offending behaviour, and providing an overall score of the risk of re-offending. It was intended that Asset would be used to aid the preparation of pre-sentence reports, supervision plans and reviews of progress. Each of these are stages in the case-management process. Asset is integrated with the electronic information systems used by YOTs so that assessments are electronically recorded and updated and available for sharing with colleagues who access the database.

The assessment tool found more favour in some YOTs than in others (Baker, 2004; Roberts et al., 2001). Some of the more influential members of OYOT were critical of the length and detail of Asset and perhaps as a result, this was one of the last aspects of evidence-based practice to find general acceptance in the service as a whole. The complaints came from those with years of experience in making assessments and writing pre-sentence reports, who found the tool more of a hindrance than help. In contrast, staff with relatively little relevant experience found that Asset helped them to keep to a structure, to be comprehensive and led to information that otherwise would not have been touched upon.

Practitioners made less use of the assessment tool for reviewing the progress of cases than had been intended. Apart from being too busy, one explanation given for this was that scores on a final Asset might compare unfavourably with scores on the initial Asset as a result of 'disclosure effects'. That is, even though progress had been made, information disclosed to the practitioner at a later stage, whether by the young person or others, would enable a more accurate and sometimes more negative assessment than had been possible earlier, giving a misleading picture of deterioration or no change. Another criticism of Asset was that it captured subjective decisions that were likely to differ from officer to officer. However, this view was partly dispelled following a workshop where it was found that differences were sometimes linked to alternative interpretations of a question and that, when everyone shared a common understanding of what the question means, the Asset responses were similar. Practice in using the assessment tool was variable, including differences in the stage at which Asset was completed (during an interview or afterwards) and in the manner of its completion (the paper version first or directly onto the YOIS version). To make appropriate use of the tool, practitioners need good assessment skills, professional training and an understanding of adolescent development.

Some dissatisfaction with Asset was linked to perceptions of it as needlessly detailed, not to benefit practice but to serve as a research tool for performance monitoring and to supply statistics for use by the YJB. The most critical practitioners objected that their judgements were being forced into tick boxes to feed the government information machine. Managerial staff in the YOT, however, found that the tool generated invaluable aggregate information, added to the YOT's database, for monitoring work and for estimating resource requirements.

Case-management

Practitioners adopted a case-management approach more by default than intention - and even then, it was not a full-blown case-management approach to the exclusion of direct one-to-one work with young people. They welcomed programmes and special projects as opportunities for the young people. Indeed, the increased availability of resources was one of the attractions of joining the YOT, and practitioners were keen that all young people should have access to the same services. However, they were concerned that reliance on programmes would interfere with the frequency and continuity of contact and thereby take away the usual opportunities to build a strong working relationship and to gain in-depth understanding. Under the old system practitioners could maintain a presence. They could see a young person all the way through the criminal process, from sitting with them in the police station after arrest and preparing the court report to regular contact throughout any ensuing court order. The disjointed involvement allowed by the case-management model made it harder for the individual practitioner to gain the trust of young people and prevented the relaxed communication that comes with familiarity. The changed nature of the relationship between worker and young person is reflected in the following lament by one former youth justice worker:

I never get a kid now dropping in to see me and saying 'Is Miss [X] in?', 'Can I have a word?', you know, when they've got a problem or they want to tell me they've done well. That whole bit seems to have gone.

The move to a case-management model left staff feeling that they no longer had as much grip on a case. They were dependant on feedback from others, but this was not always forthcoming; and with other parties involved there was less chance of them being an important support figure in that young person's life and to exercise powers of influence. Additionally, there was a risk that the young person would be treated like an object in a game of pass the parcel and would not have the opportunity to relate to anyone. Practitioners argued that the young person could get the impression that, far from having to confront the consequences of their offence and related problems, no-one was taking much notice. The danger of a case-management approach, one argued, is:

They never get to know anybody, that's my theory. That they never actually really engage with us; it's just something that they have to do...What does that tell them about their offences? It tells them that it's not really something that people want to engage with them about. It's not really a big deal: if you do this, you get this automatic response…Whereas for many young people - not all of them - their offending is problematic for them and is an expression of other problems in their lives and they actually want somebody who will engage with them and try and help them deal with those problems. And if we're not prepared to do that, what does that say to them?

However, despite such misgivings, referral to programmes became a coping strategy when officers were too busy to achieve, via one-to-one meetings, the number of contacts required by national standards. As more 'early stage' offenders were brought into the YOT's domain, case-management increasingly seemed appropriate in place of more 'hands on' work on a one-to-one level. The introduction of ISSPs in particular - requiring them to refer cases on which they had worked most intensively over a long period of time - brought home to staff in the former youth justice team that the nature of their job was different and that there would be less scope for them to carry out direct work with young people and their families. A few team members left for other jobs and remaining staff suspected that unwillingness to switch to a case-management approach had been a factor in their departure.

The transition to case-management was not as extreme as it had been in the probation service. All YOT workers still carried out some direct work with people on their caseload, to the extent that a senior member of staff felt able to describe the resulting way of working as a 'semi case-management model'. This was partly encouraged by operational managers who promoted the value of building a casework relationship. To some extent though, the latitude that staff enjoyed to exercise discretion and to prioritise one-to-one work was an outcome of staffing problems. Supervision of practitioners' work was not uniformly available and practitioners got on with the tasks that they saw as most important, as this extract indicates:

You have got an order and you can do what you like with it. Nobody is saying that you can't do this or that. You can get involved in a case as much or as little as you like…and do whatever you think you can do. I don't think I have enough time to do everything properly. My files are appalling really. Everything is in them but they need to be 'adminised' to make sure everything is in the right place at the right time. None of my Assets are on YOIS…I'm not even slightly up to date with my paperwork. I am frustrated about that but I don't know what I could leave out. You could make all your paper work look nice but you would be missing the kids out.

Although staff generally did their best to keep up with the chores of case-management, certainly their practice had not - at the time of our study, at least - been reduced to a 'korrectional karaoke' of prescribed tasks devoid of fresh thinking and professional discretion, and unconcerned with welfare (Pitts, 2001b). There had indeed been a change in working culture, but their social work had not been overwhelmed by it. In keeping with a social work ethos, staff were fundamentally helpful and caring in their stance towards each young person for whom they had responsibility and continued to regard the development of a supervisory relationship as the necessary foundation for any other work: for achieving accurate and in-depth assessment; for engaging their interest in interventions and activities; and for motivating the young person to change their behaviour.

Professional ethos

Although there was a minimum of open conflict between practitioners from the various agencies coming together into the team, there were underlying differences in their professional values and traditions. Towards the end of the formative period, the first YOT manager reflected that, while there had been some debate over details, there had indeed been a significant change in the practice: the team had 'embraced the need to prevent crime and isn't just welfare-orientated, and understands the concept of risk'. Previously, findings from the evaluation of the pilot YOTs stressed that it would be crucial for operational managers to be manifestly in favour of the change in practice culture and in harmony with their YOT manager in order to model and promote change among practitioners (Holdaway et al., 2001). Bearing this in mind, the YOT manager regretted that it had not been possible to appoint a probation officer as one of the operational managers posts, given that the probation service had taken a lead in adopting the procedures of evidence-based practice. The appointment of a police officer to the role of operational manager in one of the units had helped to promote a change of outlook in the unit where he was based. However, the operational managers and senior practitioners in the YOT were mostly from a social services background and the manager was frustrated from time to time by what Holdaway and colleagues (2001) described as 'cultural hangovers'. The manager explained that the progress of the YOT had 'come up against the dead wood syndrome of how things were done in the past'. There was a 'little cohort of staff who really don't like what is going on' and sometimes staff were not deliberately blocking development but had not fully appreciated some of the changes in legislation. In one example, former youth justice staff had argued that social services should be consulted and their approval sought whenever a child was being remanded into secure accommodation, and they had stressed that it was 'departmental policy to treat a 15 year old as vulnerable'. The YOT manager asserted that though 'it might be social services policy, it was not YOT policy' and referred them to the section in the Crime and Disorder Act that empowered magistrates to commit 15 year olds directly to custody in place of the previous requirement for them to be committed to local authority accommodation.

In contrast, another member of social services staff explained how her perspective had changed:

Researcher: *What do you think of the changes that have been made in youth justice as a result of Crime and Disorder Act?*

Practitioner: *Sometimes the traditionalist in me thinks I don't like the idea of locking up 12 year olds and all the rest of it, however when push comes to shove I find it very difficult to argue against any of the changes, I have to say. I'm surprised at myself sometimes. To give an example of that, not just the changes in the CDA but the implementation of slightly older pieces of legislation, I'm thinking particularly here of secure training orders. When that first came in I was sort of very reluctant to countenance it. I have to say now we've got three kids currently on secure training orders who would not have been, they would not have been locked up under the old legislation (they're all 14) and I have to say they probably all should be. So I think that's actually changed my mind a bit. I think that piece of legislation was right and there's nothing in the CDA really that I could argue too strongly against and quite a lot that I would argue for.*

Such overall support for the legislation was shared by most members of the team. Importantly however, this acceptance did not in any way mark a move towards a punitive, uncaring approach. That is, the adoption of case-management principles and procedures, with services differentiated according to the risk of further offending and needs for public protection, did not preclude their continuing allegiance to the 'caring credo' (Rutherford, 1993). However focused they were on offending behaviour and the consequences for victims, practitioners were always mindful of the welfare needs and rights of young people and their families, and keen to address any indications of suffering, disadvantage or discrimination. As in former youth justice practice, great store was placed on the value of forming a relationship not only as an effective means of encouraging desistance from offending but also as a matter of humanity. This key element of the caring credo was nicely expressed by one practitioner:

I still think we have got to look at that primary relationship between case-worker and kid - unpopular though it is to say it. Not what the YJB want to hear I don't think…In the end what makes a difference in the life of that child is someone sitting down and forming a relationship in staying with them through thick and thin and being consistent, and being the person who cares - because they ain't got no-one else.

Youth justice workers were already differentiating though - long before risk based case-management approaches - between cases where the person's difficulties merited such a relationship, and first or second time offenders from more stable and trouble-free backgrounds who were not expected to continue offending and where a policy of non-intervention was seen as the best way to divert them from the criminal justice system. We will look at emergent approaches for dealing with 'early stage' offending in the next chapter.

CHAPTER 5

Nipping Crime in the Bud: Interventions in the Early Stages of Offending

In considering the various preventative initiatives aimed at the early stages of offending it is necessary to draw a distinction between non-statutory preventive schemes with youngsters deemed to be at risk of offending and those measures which are a statutory response to specific anti-social or illegal behaviours. The Youth Justice Board, with national funding aimed at crime reduction and at social inclusion, has introduced various initiatives, such as programmes of activities during the school holidays known as Splash schemes and Youth Inclusion Programmes (YIPs). All of these occur outside of the judicial and legal process, and unless they take place in school, the young person's involvement is purely voluntary with the agreement of their parents or guardians (see Box 4).

In contrast, there are various pre-court interventions which have been introduced by legislation and which involve judicial procedures to decide whether or not they should be enforced. These include local child curfew orders and anti-social behaviour orders and child safety orders (see Box 5) which are legal measures, imposed and enforced through a process of law even though they do not involve court appearances. The reprimands and final warning scheme is included in this category.

Referral orders are in another category: they are a court disposal (see Box 7 in the next chapter). In this sense, they are clearly distinguishable from reprimands and final warnings. However, referral orders are similarly aimed at early stages of offending and the decisions about how the offending behaviour should be addressed take place outside the court room. In this and other respects there is common ground between final warnings and referral orders which make it appropriate to reflect on shared themes and implementation issues. This chapter therefore considers the trials and triumphs involved in introducing these two complex intervention systems aimed at the early stages of offending.

Box 4: Pre-crime prevention initiatives

Safer School Partnerships

Police officers have been placed to work in selected schools in areas with high levels of crime in order to:

- Reduce victimisation, criminality and anti-social behaviour within schools and the community.
- Work with schools on 'whole school' approaches to behaviour and discipline.
- Identify and work with children and young people at risk of becoming victims or offenders.
- Ensure the full-time education of young offenders.
- Support vulnerable children and young people through periods of change.
- Generate a safer environment in which children can learn.

Splash Schemes

School holiday crime prevention projects - were commissioned by the Home Office's Crime Reduction Programme in August 2000 and were implemented by the Youth Justice Board in areas with the highest levels of crime as a means of providing 13-16 year olds with constructive activities during school holidays. Schemes have been designed to keep teenagers occupied during school holidays by providing learning opportunities, developing social and life skills and building self-confidence and esteem.

Splash Extra

Funded by the New Opportunities Fund since summer 2002 and based on the Splash model, Splash Extra provides activities for 9-17 year olds living on estates with high levels of street crime in order to prevent street crime among young people.

Youth Inclusion Programmes (YIPs)

Implemented early 2000 in the most deprived estates across England and Wales, YIPs target 13-16 year olds who are engaged in crime or identified as at most risk of offending, truancy, school or social exclusion. The programme provides out-of-school activities in order to motivate the target group into constructive activities and back into education. The main objectives are to: reduce arrest rates in the target group by 60%; reduce recorded crime in the YIP areas by 30% and achieve at least one-third reduction in truancy and exclusions among the target group. The YJB has announced that a 32% reduction in crime in some areas and significant reductions in school exclusions that are attributed to the YIPs.

Youth Inclusion and Support Panels (YISPs)

Piloted in 14 areas since April 2003, YISPs target support to 8-13 year olds at risk of offending in order to prevent them getting involved in crime. Panel members include members of the community alongside representatives from the YOT, police, schools, health and social services. Local agencies identify and refer young people who are at high risk of offending to the panel who then consider the case and recommend a programme of support.

Box 5: Pre-court interventions

Child Curfew Order

Where children are causing distress or alarm to people living in a local community, the local authority can apply to the Home Secretary for a local child curfew order for a period of up to 90 days. Once issued, all children under ten in that local community must be in their homes by a specified time in the evening. Those found outside can be made subject to a child safety order.

Child Safety Order
Applicable to children under age 10 who have committed an offence, caused distress or harassment to others or who have breached a child curfew order. A social worker or YOT worker supervises a child who is subject to a child safety order and, in cases of non-compliance, the child can be made subject to a care order.

Acceptable Behaviour Contract (ABC)
Given when both a local authority and a YOT identify 'low level' anti-social behaviour which has been the subject of complaint in the local community. This involves agreeing a contract with the young person and their parents/carers to address the anti-social behaviour. If a young person breaches their ABC then the police or local authority can apply for an ASBO.

Anti-Social Behaviour Order (ASBO)
This order is aimed at young people over 10 years of age whose behaviour is causing distress or harassment to others who do not live in the same household. The ASBO can specify activities and places out of bounds to the young person, and non-compliance can lead to prosecution.

Reprimands and Final Warnings
First time offenders can be reprimanded. This is a formal verbal warning given by a police officer. In some cases the young person is referred to take part in a voluntary programme to address their offending behaviour. Final Warnings similarly are a formal warning given for a first or second offence, but they also include an assessment of factors associated with their offending and (usually) a programme of activities to address them, which may include a restorative 'conference' to bring all parties together in cases where the victim or victim representatives elect to attend.

The final warnings and the first sentence

In various ways the 'final warning' and the 'referral order' represent mini versions of the entire joined-up youth justice system. Both have involved the setting up of complex operational systems in which many people play a part, and calling upon almost the full gamut of joined-up services and projects. Both focus on tackling the issues that led the individual to commit the offence and involve referral to rehabilitative resources. This decision-making process takes place outside of the court room. They each lean towards 'restorative justice': that is, efforts are made to bring all relevant parties together in order that different perspectives can be shared and to discuss ways of repairing the harm done. Victims are invited to attend meetings, and even if they decline or are unable to participate, a central place is given to the victim perspective. To the extent that both these interventions combine 'punishment' with 'restorative justice' they typify an apparent ambivalence in the new youth justice.

From cautioning to final warnings

At the beginning of the 1990s the cautioning of young people was still being encouraged as 'an important way of keeping offenders out of the courts and in many circumstances reducing the risk that they will re-offend' (Home Office, 1990: 2). In some contradiction to this, government documents leading up the Crime and Disorder Act 1998 called for an end to *repeat* cautioning. Influenced by the Audit Commission's (1996) review, the White Paper stated that the youth justice services were 'weighted too heavily towards dealing with young offenders whose behaviour has been allowed to escalate out of control, rather than intervening early and effectively to prevent and reduce crime and anti-social behaviour' (Home Office, 1997: 4). The reformed system would therefore focus on 'nipping crime in the bud - stopping children at risk from getting involved in crime and preventing early criminal behaviour from escalating into persistent or serious offending' (1997: 4). The Crime and Disorder Act included several measures to achieve this including a two-stage reprimand and final warning process to replace the previous liberal cautioning system (see Box 6). This philosophy of intervening early to stop the escalation of offending was shortly afterwards extended to first time court appearances when the Youth Justice and Criminal Evidence Act 1999 introduced referral orders.

Box 6: The early intervention tariff

Sections 65 and 66 of the Crime and Disorder Act 1998 introduced a system of the single Reprimand to be followed by the Final Warning.

First time offenders can be reprimanded, finally warned or charged, depending on the seriousness of the crime.

Final warnings were introduced to bring a halt to a system of repeat cautioning. As the Home Secretary at the time put it: 'We are ending the continuous "yellow card" syndrome where offenders could be given one warning after another' (YJB Press Release, June 2000). The Audit Commission's review of the youth justice system *Misspent Youth* had acknowledged that cautioning was effective for first offenders but observed that it becomes 'progressively less effective once a pattern of offending sets in' (Audit Commission, 1996: 22). Given the well-known correlation between the number of previous convictions and the probability of reconviction, the report argued that it was crucial to determine the best point at which to move from cautioning to charging. It referred to Home Office research showing that seven out of ten who are cautioned do not reoffend within two years, but the more offences committed the higher the probability that the young person will reoffend (Home Office, 1994). The report also presented data from West Yorkshire Police indicating that three cautions was the optimum cut-off point, after which prosecution would be more effective in reducing offending (Audit Commission, 1996: 23). In the event, the second caution was chosen as the cut-off point. Thus the new system carries a message of: 'three strikes and you're in court'. In an attempt to divert young people from reaching this stage, meetings are held, sometimes with the victim present, to discuss the impact on victims and to decide a programme of interventions aimed at preventing further offending.

> *Second time offenders* cannot be given another reprimand and, unless their offence was serious enough to receive a charge, they are given a Final Warning.
>
> *Third time offenders* can only receive another final warning in exceptional circumstances, and will normally be charged. Consequently a young person who offends for the third time will normally be charged to appear in court. All young people who plead guilty for a first offence in court receive a Referral Order unless an absolute discharge or a custodial sentence are appropriate.

Referral from court to a panel

The Youth Justice and Criminal Evidence Act 1999 introduced a mandatory order for most young offenders appearing before a youth court or magistrates' court for the first time. All 10-17 year olds who plead guilty are given a referral order for a specified period of between three and 12 months - unless either an absolute discharge or a custodial or hospital order are appropriate. The disposal is so-named because it refers the offender away from the court process to a youth offender panel (YOP) set up by the local YOT.

The aim of the panel meeting is to devise a 'contract' specifying activities that are aimed at preventing further offending and providing reparation to the victim or wider community. Panels consist of one YOT member and two or more members of the community, and parents or carers are legally required to attend with their son or daughter. As in the case of final warning panels, various other parties are invited to attend, including the victim, a victim supporter and a supporter of the young person. In cases where there is no direct victim, the panel may invite someone who can bring a victim perspective to the meeting. Further meetings are held to review progress, sometimes to vary the terms of the contract, and in cases of breach. The role of the YOT member is to provide information on suitable activities and to ensure proportionality, while it is the role of the community panel members to lead the negotiations between the panel and the offender about the content of the contract. Referral orders are not treated as criminal convictions once the contract and the period of the referral order have been completed.

Referral orders were first piloted in 11 areas in England and Wales before becoming available to all courts in April 2002. The introduction of referral orders was evaluated by a consortium of universities (Newburn et al., 2002; Crawford and Newburn, 2003).

Restorative justice aspects

One of the shared characteristics by final warnings and referral orders is that they both have restorative justice elements in their procedures and intentions. While there are various models of 'restorative justice' and the concept cannot readily be pinned down, at a philosophical level at least, restorative practices are directed towards restoring the harm caused by an offence rather than towards deterrence, rehabilitation or punishment (Hoyle et al., 2002). Although an ancient form of justice that, some say, has been dominant through human history, restorative justice has risen to prominence in recent years as 'one of the most significant developments in criminal justice and criminological practice and thinking' (Crawford and Newburn, 2003:19).

Final warnings and referral orders are only partially restorative because they are mainly aimed at prevention of reoffending. Indeed, the Home Office guidance for final warnings stated that the intention behind incorporating restorative justice measures into pre-court disposals was to 'make the final warning scheme more meaningful and effective in preventing offending' (Home Office, 2001: 1). Yet the final warning system follows closely the police-led restorative cautioning procedures introduced by Thames Valley Police, and derived from a model developed in Wagga Wagga, Australia. This model makes use of a 'script' setting out statements, questions and prompts to be used by a trained facilitator. All those affected by the offence including the victim are invited to a meeting - termed a 'conference' if the victim attends - in which this script is the basis for structured dialogue. Following the theory of reintegrative shaming (Braithwaite, 1989), it is intended that these meetings will induce a sense of shame in offenders when they learn about how their offence has affected others. At the same time, offenders are treated with respect, are given a chance to express their views and are consulted about the decisions made, including decisions about how they can make amends to victims (Hoyle et al., 2002). Final warnings follow this scripted model. Initially, such meetings all took place in police stations. The Criminal Justice and Court Services Act 2000 removed the requirement for a final warning to be delivered at a police station, thus allowing a choice of alternative venues that might be more conducive to a restorative justice approach.

The restorative justice elements of referral orders are somewhat different. The dialogue is not scripted and two of the panel members are community volunteers and so have not directly been affected by the offence. Youth offending panels, rather than conferences are held. The panels may include victims and victim supporters and it is intended that the young person and their parent will be consulted.

Organising and delivering two complex schemes

The preparation and operation of final warnings and referral orders were complex logistical operations. To set them up called upon committed and efficient leadership, systematic planning and liaison with multiple parties. Once up and running, both schemes were reliant on skilled management to ensure consistency and to co-ordinate all the elements.

Delivering final warnings

OYOT was in one of the areas that had already established inter-agency links and had set up a multi-agency panel aimed at diverting young people from crime by providing appropriate interventions. It had the advantage of being in the police service area that had pioneered restorative justice cautioning in this country (Hoyle et al., 2002) and therefore the police members of the YOT were all trained and experienced in facilitating restorative cautioning. One such officer was seconded into the YOT as an operational manager and was given the task of taking plans forward for delivering final warnings. The entire first intake of staff received restorative justice training which equipped them to deliver final warnings, and two of the unit managers took on a national role as trainers of restorative justice practice to YOT workers across the country. All of this meant that the YOT made rapid progress in planning procedures and operations for delivering final warnings and in getting the process up and running. As befitted its 'pathway' status, it was identified in Youth Justice Board publications as an exemplar of good practice in delivering final warnings. OYOT claimed a low recidivism rate (9.8 per cent) for the young people who had received final warnings in the preceding 12 months. This news was encouraging but was potentially misleading given the short interval that had elapsed for most of the sample who had received final warnings up to that time. The YJB publicised the early achievements of this pathway YOT and described it as in the 'vanguard of best practice in the use of final warnings and accompanying intervention programmes' (Youth Justice Board, 2001a: 9).

The veneer of success, however, concealed various struggles and some minor in-fighting between units of the YOT as each sought to establish 'best practice' in achieving efficient procedures that met the intentions of the legislation. Given the three distinct stages involved in delivering final warnings - preparation, the final warning meeting and, usually, some rehabilitative and reparation activities - there was wide scope for variations in practice to arise. The manager of the final warning scheme prepared a guidance manual to ensure consistency across the county but staff argued that a 'one size fits all' policy does not take account of differing local circumstances nor variations in individual cases. Projects for the rehabilitation element of final warnings were not equally accessible to all parts of the county and the referral of a young person to particular projects was also affected by the biases of officers carrying out the assessments or facilitating the meetings. Moreover, once a rehabilitation programme had been agreed, its implementation could be dependent on how it was followed up by the responsible officer. One practitioner summed this up: 'Final warnings can be quite good if you're prepared to pick up doing some of the work yourself afterwards, like identifying certain issues from the assessment'. To some extent therefore, the rehabilitation programme which the young person received depended on their 'luck of the draw' in which officer was allocated to their case.

Delivering referral orders

The introduction of referral orders took an even greater toll on the time of staff than final warnings. The idea of referral orders found favour among the practitioners and OYOT was proud to be one of the pilot areas. However, the investment of time and effort it demanded and the problems to which it gave rise generated a lot of strong feelings and, across the YOT, a love-hate relationship developed with this radically different way of responding to first court appearances. As with final warnings, referral orders soaked up a lot of the resources aimed more widely at both pre-court and post-court disposals. There was such a focus on obtaining whatever was needed for referral orders that it came to be described as a 'Rolls Royce service' when set against other relatively less well-resourced and smoothly running services.

A full-time volunteer co-ordinator was appointed to recruit volunteers, find venues and to co-ordinate the various meetings for YOPs. Recruiting volunteers and identifying venues involved skilful networking and use of snowballing processes. The co-ordinator began by targeting people who were not only receptive to offering help but who also provided useful information about suitable venues for youth offender panels and potential sources of volunteers. Community safety officers 'bent over backwards' to help and to share their working knowledge. These contacts were helpful in speeding up developments. The co-ordinator set out to target groups that are usually less well represented among volunteers including young men, minority ethnic people, and residents in high crime areas. For example, a mobile police unit which visited a high crime area was used to attract local residents into getting involved in the delivery of referral orders. Various sources of publicity were used such as local newsletters and community centres and local radio. The aim was to recruit one or two people from appropriate groups who would then cascade information about the work to acquaintances and friends.

Enthusiasm among staff for referral orders was tinged with the inevitable worries about the ensuing workload. Front-line staff welcomed what looked like an opportunity to extend restorative justice work, which so far was largely associated with final warnings and the reparative elements of other court orders. Some saw referral orders as the most radical aspect of all the youth justice reforms because of the involvement of community members in the decision making process:

> I was very enthusiastic about referral orders. I knew that if we get it right it is going to be the most significant change we have had, not just for the youth justice agencies but for the country.

However, getting the process up and running proved to be what many described as a 'bureaucratic nightmare'. It was understandably difficult to succeed in getting all parties together at the right time in the right place and then holding youth offending panels that conformed to the intended policy. Various complications ensued. Young people and their parents or supporters often had difficulty in understanding what was required of them; there were disputes over the relative roles of panel members; and venues were difficult to secure.

In the early stages of delivering referral orders, before experience had been accumulated, panel members were inexperienced and were prone to make mistakes or behave inappropriately. YOT officers who acted as panel advisers spoke of how unprofessional some panel meetings had seemed. Practitioners were concerned that panel members occasionally behaved like sentencers and treated the YOT officer as the equivalent of a magistrate's clerk. In these 'kangaroo courts' decisions were made without seeking the views of the young person and their parents.

In other instances, problems in conducting panel discussions occurred because of unsuitable venues in noisy locations. For example, one practitioner described a panel meeting which was held simultaneously with an aerobic class in the neighbouring room, resulting in an experience in which 'the whole panel was bouncing up and down and we couldn't hear ourselves speak'. Such difficulties could not always have been anticipated when the venues were selected, but showed the importance of visiting premises in advance before reserving them for this purpose.

Delays in setting up panels could occur at several stages in the process: securing the venue; making contact with victims; explaining the process to victims and giving them the opportunity to reply or provide a statement; making arrangements for the young person and their carer to attend; contacting supporters of victims and of offenders; and organising a date and time that suited everybody. Unsurprisingly, therefore, it was fairly common for significant delays to occur. In the worst cases the duration of the referral order could be a third of the way through and the young person was still waiting for the panel to meet. During such a long wait there is no official reason for contact with the young person who is therefore left in limbo and, in the absence of support, at some risk of reoffending before the referral order has developed beyond being nominal.

Thus, staff involved in the piloting of referral orders who had begun with great enthusiasm became frustrated and disappointed as the administrative burdens and the procedural complexities became more manifest, and in response to the disproportionate 'contract' of activities which young people were receiving for relatively minor offences.

Bringing in the victim

In recent years there has been a growing conviction among commentators and politicians that victims should be offered a greater role within criminal justice processes. Whereas traditionally victims were described as the 'forgotten party', they are now more likely than ever to be listened to by the various agencies of the criminal justice system, as well as to be catered for by voluntary-based support structures. As part of this movement, a significant difference between 'old' and 'new' youth justice, is the increased attention to the victim through the inclusion of victim statements in court reports and, more directly, through their attendance at final warning conferences and referral order panels.

The objectives of victim attendance are multiple. First, victims are given an opportunity to tell the offender about the effect the offence has had on them and for this to be recognised and acknowledged by the offender. Second, young offenders are confronted with the consequences of their offending behaviour and the harm caused and are subsequently encouraged to take responsibility for their actions. Third, it enables victims to address concerns or questions they may have by meeting the offender face-to-face so that they can gain a better understanding of their attitudes and why the offence occurred, as well as assess the probability of the crime reoccurring. Finally, it provides an opportunity for victims to receive some kind of emotional or material reparation (Crawford and Newburn, 2003).

A victim liaison officer was appointed to the YOT to help integrate victim issues into youth justice services. The YOT manager decided that there should be a member of the team who was 'dedicated to the victim perspective' and who would 'give us a hard time if we neglect the needs of victims'. The job description broadly concerned all issues relating to victim contact but, more specifically, she was required to ensure that procedures for involving victims - obtaining victim statements and inviting participation in meetings - were sensitive and informed. Other aspects of the victim liaison officer's role were to provide information to YOT officers about victim issues and to be involved in developing staff awareness of the needs and rights of victims. It was ironic that, despite being a former employee of Victim Support, the victim liaison officer was not permitted to initiate contact with victims because of data protection regulations: only police officers had this authorisation. As the procedures for delivering final warnings and referral orders tightened up and national guidelines were refined, the victim liaison officer and a team of sessional workers played an increasingly important role in obtaining victim statements and in facilitating the participation of victims and relaying information back to them.

For and against victim inclusion

Although the intention of the final warning scheme was that all victims would be given the option of attending a final warning conference, it soon became apparent that the majority of victims opted out of attending. At the same time, it became clear that the number of young people being referred for final warnings was much higher than anticipated. It was therefore decided to speed up the process by adopting a 'one-stop approach' for cases where the victim had indicated that they would not want to attend - that is, most cases. This was achieved by issuing the final warning straight after the assessment had been carried out. While this obviously speeded up the process and boosted the numbers of final warnings delivered within the target periods, some staff believed that it undermined the potential of the process to be restorative. It meant that victim refusal to participate might be, in one sense, welcomed and it discouraged alternative efforts to encourage or facilitate their participation, especially in the case of those who might be hesitant and need time to think about it.

YOT officers formed the impression that young people were more affected by their final warning and less likely to re-offend when the victim attended the final warning meeting. Even if the victim did not want to participate in a meeting, a discussion of the views of victims helped to ensure the delivery of a 'restorative' warning. This is in accordance with research showing the value of victim participation, if not by their direct presence then in the form of indirect communication between victims and offenders, the use of accurate victim statements and feeding back information about the session and its outcome to the victim (Hoyle, 2002).

A spokesperson for Victim Support suggested that the organisation was agnostic about prospects of referral orders being helpful:

> The value and potential for referral orders is to do something completely different that could never have been done before in that semi-judicial way, opening all kinds of doors. Whether the conferencing exercise will be something constructive for the victim and the local community and the offender in repairing harm remains to be seen. All that has such potential and for lay people to be able to take over the responsibility for panels is quite exciting. But it's also quite unsettling.

The same spokesperson thought that phoning up victims to ask them to suggest an appropriate form of reparation not intended for them personally was placing an unacceptable burden onto them and was tantamount to turning the victim into a sentencer.

The majority of victims approached by the YOT did not want to attend meetings with the offender. In some cases they may be opting out because they have not been given enough information to make an informed choice. It is generally agreed that more victims would attend if they were given better preparation (Hoyle et al., 2001). Research on restorative cautioning for young adults found that if facilitators gave misleading messages to victims they would be unlikely to turn up (Hoyle et al., 2001).

There are, however, some clear instances where victims may be keen to attend but where their contribution would be contrary to restorative justice objectives. Victims may use the opportunity inappropriately to try to punish or 'scare straight' the young person. While the victim may feel better after such a meeting it would be unlikely to be constructive and the effect would be the antithesis of restorative justice. Others may decline to attend because they are sceptical that such a meeting is viable or, as in the case of this victim, because they are still too distressed and angry about what was done to them:

We weren't told the date when he was up in court. The next thing we heard is that we had got a letter from these Youth people saying 'Would we talk to him?' The same day we got a phone call, asking would we like to meet him face to face and I said 'Not really'...I mean my temper wouldn't last that long if I saw him. And she said 'well it is to get him to face his own responsibility, to talk it over'...You couldn't do it with him. With him you would be wasting your time. He would go out of the door and he would have a grin on his face and he will just laugh at you... I think that people do make mistakes when they are younger and that a six months supervision order for somebody that has made a mistake and who can learn by their mistakes is right. People have to have an opportunity to improve and show remorse. But this guy isn't in that category! To me, I don't want anything to do with him. I don't want him anywhere near me. It will take me a long while to get over this. I'll never forget it.

While it is possible that some victims do not attend because they have not been properly advised of the purpose, others may impose their own interpretation onto the purpose and value of such meetings, as the following interview extract conveys:

I was invited to a tribunal. I think it was going to have the offenders and me and the police and, the urm, I can't remember her name. So we were all going to get together. They weren't, at that stage, going to know what their sentence was going to be. I said at the time: 'I'm not sure how much good I will be because I am not that good at eyeballing a young lad and saying: If you come near my place again I will skin you'...I chatted to some friends about it and they said: 'It is a good idea because you will then know them and they will know you and you are going to see them around in town and they are going to leave you alone'. So I then decided that yes I would try and go to that.

The victim in this instance was subsequently disappointed that he was not informed when the meeting took place. Policies for filtering out unsuitable victims, if such policies exist, were not made clear.

The perspective of victims

In our role as evaluators, we interviewed victims, analysed victim questionnaires and observed a number of conferences to learn about restorative processes from the perspective of victims. Although the small number of victims we interviewed (19) does not allow firm conclusions to be drawn, detailed qualitative interviews raised questions about the adequacy of provision made for victims before, during and after conferences. In particular, there were various ways in which the victims seemed to have lacked good preparation prior to the conference, with the result that they had incorrect expectations or were surprised by what occurred. The following account from the parent of an eight year old victim of violence by two older boys illustrates some issues where there was scope for better preparation of victims participating in a final warning conference:

> Father of victim: *We were told they were just kids playing a prank…When I saw them, I was quite taken aback because they weren't children, they were youths. And I was angry. It was a surreal situation to be up and to sit there as though we were discussing a holiday let's say…Well the reason we took part in it was to let our boys see that they weren't monsters these other two. But in the process of doing that, I felt we were being fed the wrong sort of information, because of what was coming back from the youth offending team. There were a few things I wasn't happy with. One of them was, we were told 'when you come for the meeting, you will be the first there. They will have to walk in after you'. That wasn't the case. They were already there, they were sat there relaxed and we had to walk into that. So I thought well, it wasn't that we were late, we were on time, in fact we were slightly early.*

> Mother of victim: *The impression I got from [the facilitator] was that…he was wanting to get them off as lightly as possible…And he just seemed to be so impressed with their families…I think the whole attitude was wrong. And it was geared towards, y'know, these really good families…He was looking after them. It was outrageous, I just didn't want to be there. It was a very one-sided thing and we just had to go along with it I felt in the end, we were just pulled along.*

In another example, the reverse applied. Good preparation and skilled handling by the facilitator made it easier for the victim to attend a conference and prepared him much more fully for the experience, with favourable results:

> Victim: *I was a bit pessimistic about going to the police station…even up to the time that I got there, but he [the facilitator] made me feel relaxed.*
> Researcher: *What did he tell you about it before you went?*

Victim: *He come out to see me and he had that script that he used...and he more or less went through that, what would go on and that, so as I knew what was going to go on...it was nearly an hour I suppose he spent with me going through all that script, and explaining everything.*

Researcher: *And did that make you feel more confident about going?*

Victim: *It was good, him coming up and having a chat. It makes you feel more relaxed, and then they ring you up to make sure you're going to be there. I felt confident about going to it, but I was still, you know, pessimistic about what it was going to be like. Is it going to be any repercussions from them to us? You know getting in touch with their mates, saying 'I met our neighbours at the police station' or them getting their mates to go and do something. This is the only thing about being a sort of witness. That was the only thing I was a bit dubious of.*

Researcher: *So you went to the conference. Was it useful?*

Victim: *I thought it was very good, yes, to meet the girls and to talk to them and also to talk to their parents, I think that done a lot of good.*

Researcher: *Why do you think that?*

Victim: *I just don't know, just something about it I thought was good, meeting the girls, and being able to talk to them face-to-face instead of just seeing them in the street or something, it's different.*

Researcher: *Did it change how you feel about the crime committed against you?*

Victim: *I suppose it does really, yes...To know that the girls were sorry for what they done, in that respect yeah.*

Researcher: *Did it change how you feel about the person offended against you?*

Victim: *I think it did really, yes, because I found them as two quite nice girls when you spoke to them...which I think goes a long way...I thought it went very, very well to be honest. I hope I didn't go over the top in saying to the girls if I see you I don't hold any grudges against you for doing this, and if I see you in the street I don't want you to ignore me, you should speak to me or I'll speak to you.*

The main source of complaint from victims concerned a lack of communication. For example, victims had not been informed about outcomes nor been contacted to see if the promised reparation activities had actually taken place. Others would have valued follow-up contact to discuss their strong feelings aroused during and after the event; that might have been an appropriate point at which to refer them to Victim Support.

Formalising a victim policy

The intended integration of work with victims into youth justice services gave rise to frequent questions from YOT practitioners about what they or other staff were allowed to do in relation to work with victims, and about what the proper procedures were and how their activities fitted into other policies. The YJB produced a set of guidelines for YOTs on developing victim policies, and a consultant, who was already carrying out work for Victim Support, was appointed to chair a group to discuss and develop the

YOT's victim policy. On finalising the policy document, the chair of the group concluded that the policy would help ensure that victims were not seen as peripheral to the work of the YOT:

> *I've had discussions with [the YOT manager and deputy manager] and they clearly are very committed to making sure the victims get a good deal. It's not just a commitment to a kind of an ideal...but has to be implemented strategically...and this policy will hopefully help.*

Do early interventions 'nip crime in the bud'?

Have the final warning and referral order schemes helped to achieve the YJB's aim of 'nipping crime in the bud'? Some early research findings provided tentative support for the value of final warnings in preventing further offending. In a one-year follow-up of 856 final warnings, it was found that the overall rate of further proceedings for the final warning group was 30 per cent - six percentage points lower than the expected rate of further proceedings, based on comparison with the rate of further proceedings after one year for a group of 4,718 offenders who had been cautioned in 1998 (Hine and Celnick, 2001). Referral orders came into operation later and qualitative data are not available. However, the evaluators of referral orders pilots in 11 areas concluded that 'the referral order and youth offender panel, for all the difficulties associated with their implementation, hold real promise for greater involvement of young people's families, the victims of crime and the wider community and for more constructive, deliberative, inclusive and participative ways of responding to youthful offending' (Crawford and Newburn, 2003: 237).

Critics of early intervention have characterised it as 'not benign', in contrast to 'intermediate treatment' during the 1970s, and have argued that 'appeals to correctional, punitive and deterring priorities for its legitimacy...in the final analysis, will serve only to criminalise the most structurally vulnerable children' (Goldson, 2000). Left realists predicted that the final warning system would result in inappropriate custodial sentences because too many early stage offenders would be appearing in court (Pitts, 1998). The worst fears of practitioners have tended to endorse such concerns. While YOT staff welcomed the restorative justice elements of final warnings and referral orders as 'meaningful interventions confronting kids with what they have done, and getting in there to do some good work at an early stage', they also saw them as escalating more young people up the sentencing ladder if the potential benefits of early intervention did not work overnight. The general concern is that the more interventions are used early on in a young person's offending career the quicker the range of community options will be exhausted, increasing the likelihood of a custodial sentence. Any such pattern is likely to be exacerbated by the YJB performance measure which requires the majority of final warnings (80 per cent by 2004) to include an intervention.

Staff ambivalence towards final warnings also applied to referral orders. For both these disposals they were conscious of the potential for both harm and good to arise depending on how they were implemented. Crawford and Newburn's description of the referral order as a 'peculiar hybrid attempt to integrate restorative justice ideas and values into youth justice practice [within] a clearly coercive, penal context' (2003: 239) could equally be applied to final warnings. As we discuss in the next chapter, this combination also touched the considerations of sentencers within the transformed youth justice as they sought to make sense of the new legislation.

CHAPTER 6

The Decision of the Court

The 'youth court', which was known as the 'juvenile court' until 1992, is a specialised version of the magistrates' court which tries defendants under the age of 18. Since the Children and Young Persons Act 1933, it has had a statutory duty 'to have regard to the welfare of the child' when reaching its decisions. This chapter draws on interviews with YOT staff and magistrates sitting in the 'youth court', plus observations of court proceedings, to consider how the reforms to the youth justice system have touched on their role and their perspectives of the legislation introduced by the Crime and Disorder Act 1998 and the Youth Justice and Criminal Evidence Act 1999. Although youth courts now have a lot more orders to dispense it is debatable whether they have more power or whether it has a more effective role.

New sentencing options and powers

Both YOT staff and magistrates welcomed the range of sentences available in contrast to the previously restricted sentencing options (see Box 7). Faced with an array of new orders which had a specified purpose, magistrates anticipated much more scope for appropriate sentencing in contrast to a situation where they had been 'dishing out endless conditional discharges or supervision orders' with little confidence that they would achieve anything. They also welcomed greater powers to deal with young offenders themselves rather than commit them to the crown court.

In practice though, once the new legislation came into force, the prescriptiveness as to which disposal should be imposed in which circumstances gave rise to continuing frustration. As one magistrate noted:

I sometimes wonder why are we bothering to be here...Everything is pre-arranged and it could be done by pressing a button on a computer.

On the other hand, more experienced magistrates felt able to regard instructions in their Youth Court Bench Book as guidelines from which they could deviate on occasions if they did not seem appropriate. An example of this occurred in one of the court sessions which the researchers observed. In two cases, conditional discharges were given to young people subject to referral orders but who had re-offended. The bench members later explained to us that they knew this went against instructions but, in their view, there had been no other option because the referral order panel meetings had been delayed. While they thought that a newly trained person would probably 'go by the book', their previous experience had given them the confidence to use their judgement. Unfortunately, such exercising of discretion introduces inconsistencies in sentencing that are likely to be perceived as differential treatment and the defendants' good or bad fortune in coming before a particular bench on a particular day.

Box 7: New court disposals for children and young people

Referral Orders

Introduced by the Youth and Criminal Evidence Act 1999, referral orders became available to all courts from April 2002. Most young offenders aged 10-17 years old appearing in court for the first time who plead guilty, unless the charge is serious enough to warrant custody, are referred to a youth offender panel drawn from the local community and facilitated by the YOT. The panel agrees a contract with the young person and their parents or guardian and the order lasts between three to 12 months depending on the seriousness of the offence. (An amendment was introduced in 2003 allowing courts to give a conditional discharge or a fine for non-imprisonable first offences).

Action Plan Orders

This sentence provides a short intensive community-based programme combining punishment, rehabilitation and reparation. The order lasts for three months and is designed to address the risks and needs of the young person. It can include repairing the harm done to the victim or the community, education and training or attending programmes designed to address offending behaviour.

Reparation Orders

Reparation orders aim to make young offenders face up to their crimes and take responsibility for the consequences of their actions. This can involve apologising in person and making direct reparation to the victim or to the wider community such as repairing criminal damage. Any reparation carried out may last for a maximum of 24 hours and carried out over a maximum period of three months. Additional arrangements introduced in 2001 enable courts to specify a second option of 'community payback' in cases where there was no specified victim or where the victim does not wish to have further contact with the offender. Activities in which the offender can 'put something back into the community' are specified, for example removing graffiti or repairing damaged property.

Parenting Orders

Parenting orders are considered by the court in every case and require a parent or carer of a child who has been convicted of an offence to attend counselling or guidance sessions and comply with specified requirements. The order may also be applied to parents who have failed to secure their child's attendance at school.

Detention and Training Orders

DTOs require the young offender (aged 12-17) to be subject to a period of detention followed by a period of supervision in the community. The length of the sentence can be between four months and two years. The aim is to reduce the risk of re-offending by providing a clear focus on planned and constructive use of time spent in custody and effective supervision and support after release.

Curfew Orders

This sentence requires a young person to remain for set periods of time at a specified place. The time can range between two-12 hours a day and the sentence can last for no more than six months for those aged 16 years and above, and three months for those under 16 years of age.

Supervision Orders

A supervision order can last up to three years and a range of 'specified activities' can be attached to this order (such as participation in the ISSP) when the sentence is used for more serious offences. A young person receiving a supervision order is also required to take part in activities set by the YOT which could include repairing the harm done by their offence either to the victim or the community and attending offending behaviour programmes.

There were, perhaps inevitably, some teething problems in the administration of the new court orders. Panel members thought that the specifications did not match the realities and that some of the complications could have been avoided. For example, there was a lack of clarity about procedures to follow in the event of breaches. Their frustrations were shared by YOT practitioners. Referral orders and parenting orders in particular were identified as problematic.

Referral orders have presented a main exception to the general increase in sentencing scope. Our 'pathway' YOT was one of those which piloted the referral order before it was brought into general use in 2002 and the criteria for imposing referral orders were seen as limiting choice in sentencing. Indeed, the introduction of referral orders had the effect of taking away from them, in the case of first court appearance, some of the additional options so recently put in place by the CDA. Reparation orders and action plan orders were subsequently used less frequently. The option of conditional discharge which YOT staff and magistrates regarded as an effective sentence was taken away and only exceptional cases could be given an absolute discharge. Magistrates found this three-way choice to be over-limiting, resulting in the imposition of the same sentence - a referral order - for relatively minor offences, such as 'drunk and disorderly' and for more serious offences, such as 'actual bodily harm'.[2]

YOT officers and magistrates were alarmed by the increasing number of young people receiving referral orders for minor offences when they had not even previously received a final warning. This occurred if they had denied responsibility for an offence and only admitted it when it had reached the stage of a court appearance or after being found guilty. YOT officers gave these examples to illustrate the need for some flexibility to be introduced:

---

[2]Following an amendment in 2003, in the case of relatively minor offences, sentencers were able to use their discretion on whether to impose a referral order or alternatively a conditional discharge or a fine.

We've had a recent example of somebody who'd got no previous cautions, nicked a 99p felt tip pen with some friends, but he got caught and his friends phoned him up on his mobile and told him not to admit anything. So he denied it and he had to go to court. Went to court, mortified, admitted it and got a three month referral order. I don't really know what we're supposed to do with him apart from tell him to choose his friends a bit better. There should be some flexibility to go back to a reprimand or a final warning and there isn't because the final warning guidelines say once you're in court, that's it.

You have cases where neighbours' sons both get referral orders but in one case it's for something minor and in the other it's more serious. It sends the wrong message to parents. They think 'Well if my son goes to a referral order panel for committing a serious ABH how come next door's son is going for a drunk and disorderly? We're trying to tell our son this is serious but other young people go for relatively minor things'.

Such apparent anomalies may have been exacerbated by an increase in the number of children and young people pleading 'not guilty'. Magistrates were under the impression that there had been an increase in the number of trials for those appearing in court for the first time and attributed this to solicitors advising them to plead not guilty. Referral orders are not popular with lawyers because young people receiving them cannot be legally represented at the subsequent meeting with the youth offending panel, and so there may have been some basis to this supposition. An unfortunate consequence of this situation is that a young person, who initially denies but subsequently admits responsibility for an offence, is then catapulted onto a referral order, even though they had not previously been reprimanded or received a final warning. The general consensus was that it would have been better if magistrates had been allowed greater flexibility in applying referral orders in order to avoid three months input from hard-pressed YOT staff when a conditional discharge was suitable, and, in other instances where the offence had been more serious, so that an alternative to a DTO could be imposed.

It should be noted though that none of the magistrates were opposed to decisions about the content of a referral order being a matter for the panel rather than themselves. Like YOT staff, they applauded the inclusion of members of the public in youth offending panels. The following extract was typical of comments made about referral orders:

The idea of trying to get the community itself to be involved, and of getting the community itself to impose the 'sentence' is I think an excellent idea because it is peer group pressure, it is society. It is that kind of pressure, which if anything is going to have some effect on these children rather than us sitting there and spouting out at them, as we sometimes do.

While decisions about the content of referral orders obviously take place outside of the court domain (see Chapter 4 for a discussion of the youth offender panels and referral order contracts), the part played by the court in imposing them and in responding to breaches is affected by administrative complications. In particular, when there are delays in organising panels and young people re-offend, this presents the courts with the problem of responding appropriately to the subsequent offence. Such delays are commonplace and can occur for a variety of reasons: finding a suitable venue, contacting victims, making the necessary arrangements for all parties to attend. Magistrates were concerned about the number of applications being made to extend referral orders, especially because they had been advised only to grant such extensions in exceptional cases. In one of the hearings that we observed a second extension was given for the same referral order. While magistrates were somewhat exasperated by the delays, they accepted explanations from the YOT that the reasons have been out of their control. Another criticism has been a lack of clarity about the correct breaching procedure.

The attention we have given here to dissatisfactions arising from referral orders reflects the emphasis that was given to these issues in our discussions with magistrates and YOT staff about the legislation. The instructions for imposing parenting orders - though less prescriptive than referral orders - also placed magistrates under pressure to impose a sentence in some situations when it does not seem appropriate and may risk doing more harm than good. Consequently, there were fewer parenting orders arising from proceedings in the youth court than was expected, even though panels are required to consider the need for a parenting order in every case. Magistrates were frequently faced with what was described as a 'conundrum'. Either the parent was already trying and 'doing all the things that a parenting order requires' so that a court order would seem unnecessary and punitive, or the relationship between the young person and parent was so strained that imposing an order would risk exacerbating that. In some cases, they were advised that the parent was incapable of keeping to the terms of an order because of severe alcohol or drug use, and in other cases they were informed that arrangements had already been made for the parent to attend a group or receive support on a voluntary basis. Practitioners viewed parenting orders as stigmatising and unhelpful and therefore rarely recommended them.

In those rare cases where a parenting order was imposed, there were uncertainties about the procedure to follow when the parent breached it. Whereas breaches of community orders would normally be simply reported to the police who would then instigate court proceedings, neither the police nor the Crown Prosecution Service knew what procedures should be followed and delays occurred. No doubt, the well-publicised imprisonment in May 2002 of a parent who was in breach of a parenting order, will have encouraged all parties in this county, and elsewhere in the country, to clarify such procedures.

The purpose of sentencing

In some parts of the country there was an alarming increase in the use of custody following the watershed of the Crime and Disorder Act 1998. Oxfordshire was one such area: during the first year of the YOT's operation the custody rate was almost 10 per cent compared to a national average of four per cent. The YJB counting rules at the time may have inflated this statistic but it fitted with staff perceptions that custody was 'overused'. In particular, there were concerns that custody was being used with a younger age group.

Such statistics have, of course, been linked to the debate about the increased punitiveness of the new legislation. Yet, in our discussions with magistrates, they were clear that they were interested in sentences that would steer young people away from further involvement in crime: 'Stopping them offending is the be all and end all'. Towards this goal, they had been impressed by the promotion of DTOs as training programmes that continued post-release, but they all emphasised that the imposition of a custodial sentence was always a last resort.

Practitioners largely viewed custodial sentences as a destructive experience for young people and to be avoided if possible. A key concern was that youth court panels were not making allowance for the likelihood that, with the end of repeat cautioning, young people are now likely to appear before the court sooner in their 'offending career' than they would otherwise have done. This quicker entry to the court system would then be followed by an acceleration through different sentences because of the faster processing of court proceedings in general. A young person could reach the point of a custodial sentence very rapidly, especially if sentencers did not take account of 'the reality that for some young people it can take quite a long time to change their behaviour' and for interventions to 'take hold'.

Our discussions with magistrates revealed that they were enthusiastic about 'restorative justice', if a little hazy about its meaning, but did not see court appearances or even punishment as at odds with such an approach. What they wanted was orders that would work in reducing offending though without being in conflict with welfare considerations. Some pointed to punishment as a means to this end, as the following discussion with two magistrates illustrates:

Researcher: *Do you think that the new legislation presents any conflict with the need to consider the welfare of young people?*

Magistrate 1: *I think welfare probably is paramount. But then it is not just the welfare of the child. It is the welfare of the community. There is a balance, but at the same time, there are very few of us who would look upon punishment for punishment's sake. I hope none of us. Because you are looking at the broader picture of how can we stop this young person offending, and how can we make them into a person that doesn't need to or doesn't wish to.*

Magistrate 2: *Punishment is always used as a last resort isn't it? If punishment is needed it is coming after we've tried everything else. I was appointed at about the same time as the 'short sharp shock' was introduced and that didn't work, and there is no reason in some respects why it should. With the recent changes I think there has been a welcome shift towards trying to be constructive rather than dishing out punishment. And so, by implication, it must be that we are looking more towards the welfare of the child.*

Magistrate 1: *Yes, but that's not to say that a young person does not get the appropriate punishment. But one hopes there is a constructive arm to it rather than purely the punitive arm.*

Perhaps in this they share the view of Antony Duff, professor of philosophy at Stirling University, that restoration can be achieved through punishment - albeit punishment that is conceptualised as a 'communicative enterprise that addresses the wrongdoer...as someone for whom we care...' and helps them to 'recognise the wrongs they have done, as wrongs; to see the need for apologetic reparation to those they have wronged - the need to restore the relations that their crime damaged; and to embark (with our help) on the necessary task of self-reform' (Duff, 2002: 133). In treating juveniles as possessing agency they are to be regarded as 'neither so immature that they can certainly not be held criminally responsible, nor so mature that they are certainly as fit as any other adult to be held criminally responsible' (2002: 116).

The idea of a court appearance and penalty as educational spilled over into criticisms of the adversarial system and the role of solicitors in encouraging 'not guilty' pleas. It was clear from the following comment that there was some adherence to the principle that young people should be 'confronted with the consequences of their behaviour' rather than let off the hook:

I'm a bit sad that solicitors now prompt their clients to wriggle out of things if there is any possibility. I think for youths it would be much better to have the old fashioned solicitors who, if they knew that the young person had done this thing, encouraged them to hold their hands up and say 'I'm sorry I did it.' You know and then put up some mitigation. But I do quite often feel now that if there is the least possibility of providing some sort of 'wriggle out' that they will encourage the child to give no comment. It's actually better if you're a young person and you're caught in the act to say 'yes I did do it, it was me on this motorbike' or 'I'm the person who burgled the house' - whatever it is. It's actually better for that child's character to get on with it and take the consequences than to be encouraged by adults to wriggle out of it. So there! (laughing).

Similarly, longer standing magistrates were pleased that the new legislation gave them more powers to deal with under-14 year olds and viewed the removal of *doli incapax* as a realistic response to an increase in 'street-wise young people who know how to play the system', for example, twelve year olds who breached bail conditions knowing that they could not be remanded in custody. To some extent magistrates seemed resigned to 'widening the net' but thought that these measures were 'the only answer to the way behaviour has changed'.

The efficiency and culture of court proceedings

A large proportion of the YOT's activities revolve around the work of the courts, both in providing information to assist magistrates with their judicial deliberations and in administering and supervising the penalties and sentences which they decide to impose. The provision of high quality pre-sentence reports and other information by court duty officers was an important source of job satisfaction for YOT staff requiring expertise and professionalism. YOT officers took pride in the quality of their pre-sentence reports and applied a gate-keeping system, challenging each other should a report slip through that did not fulfil the guidelines imposed. Report preparation required a detailed assessment procedure, yet staff had succeeded in preparing most reports within the time limits stipulated by YJB national standards. Magistrates were impressed by this quick production of reports even though staff were conspicuously working at full stretch. Indeed, they expressed an overall appreciation of the service they received from the team of YOT workers, comparing them favourably with the former youth justice team. They were seen as now more purposeful and, as a team, more balanced in their perspectives. Nevertheless they had occasionally been aware of a fall in standards following the in-take of staff with no prior experience of court work. After an intake of unqualified support staff operational managers acknowledged that because of staff shortages they had on occasion 'sent in inexperienced staff who really don't know what they are doing in court'.

Once the orders have been imposed, it is the job of others to 'make them happen'. A feature of most new orders is that they are complex and multi-faceted and they are likely to involve other parties and agencies in addition to the YOT and the young person. Arranging for all parties to play their part within the time allotted makes steep demands on a YOT officer's time and can involve complicated logistics. Such administrative complexities apply particularly to referral orders and, to a lesser extent, action plan orders. YOT staff were not sure that magistrates always appreciated the steps involved and the number of potential obstacles to realising the courts' decisions, nor the extent to which they were driving the orders along by working to motivate the young person and to keep them to task:

> *I think the thought with some people is that you can have a panel or a final warning conference, fill in all your referral forms and post them off and it will all happen by magic. But of course it doesn't. You have to chase it up and take kids places and make sure they get there and make sure they understand what they have to do...And when that doesn't happen then it doesn't work does it? You can make it work: you can make anything work but you have to do it!*

> *[Court orders] are a lot of work, and that seems to be unrecognised. There are still things in these kids' lives that need sorting out and it requires a hell of a lot of work to do that.*

Speeding up the process

The call for reform of the youth justice system gave particular attention to the need to shorten the time taken to process young offenders from arrest to sentence. *No More Excuses* made the point that 'Delays in the youth justice system can frustrate and anger victims and give young offenders the impression that they can offend with impunity' and declared that halving the time this typically takes was to be a 'top priority'(Home Office, 1997c: 4). The logic of bringing offence and penalty closer together by speeding up the administration of prosecution and court proceedings was welcomed by magistrates, but resulted in considerable pressure for themselves as well as for YOT staff.

In Oxfordshire, less than a third of magistrates had been trained as youth magistrates and the new demands meant that 'the clerk has not been able to get enough people to man the courts'. Some of the youth court panel therefore found themselves sitting about twice the recommended number of times over the course of a year. The piloting of referral orders, in particular, had placed an increased burden on the panel and was particularly onerous coming so soon after the introduction of other new penalties.

Throughout this demanding and busy time magistrates duly attended training and induction sessions and were 'constantly worked on about getting things through'. Longer-serving magistrates observed that they had raised their expectations of others and had switched from typically obliging requests for more time to a habit of putting pressure on others to get a move on, as is well illustrated in the following comment:

The thing that we are doing much more as a bench is stating at a court adjournment what we expect to happen before the next hearing. So we have an expectation that at the next hearing we expect to do so and so. It is much more structured. Whereas at one time we might have said: 'You asked for two weeks. Do you want four?' now it's: 'You want three weeks, we'd like it to be two'. As a result we are not getting asked for nearly as many what I would call spurious adjournments as we were getting in the past. This isn't just with the Youth Court, but youth in particular. There is more a feeling of momentum in the court, whilst not losing sight of the fact that the most important thing is to be just.

Case tracking meetings were regularly held to identify cases which were getting left behind and should therefore be treated as urgent. Various ways of increasing efficiency and saving time were identified. For example, the police put in place procedures to distinguish an arrest warrant for a persistent young offender (PYO) from other arrest warrants so that these could be treated more urgently.

It was noted with regret, though, that fast tracking and speeding up the administration of court proceedings had brought some disadvantages. In particular, sometimes cases were heard and sentences imposed before there had been time for a victim impact statement to be obtained. Further examples are discussed in Chapter 8.

The court ethos

Youth courts are now required to be less formal and more friendly places in which to deal with defendants. The White Paper *No More Excuses* states that 'the government…sees a need for a more fundamental reform to change the culture of the youth court, making it more open and accessible, engaging offenders and their families more closely and giving a greater voice to victims' (Home Office, 1997c: 3). Subsequently, a Home Office 'demonstration project' was carried out in two areas. It recommended the use of friendly dialogue to engage the young people and their carers, and seating arrangements which decreased the distance between magistrates and others (Allen et al., 2000).

Some magistrates were rather irritated by the suggestion that the manner in which youth courts were conducted needed to be reformed so that they would be more appropriate for children and young people. They pointed out that they had already been following such practices but that this had not been recognised. The following indicates that such objections were fairly widespread:

Magistrate A: *I went to the YJB conference and a great fuss was made there about how the courts should be arranged. But of course we've been like this for years. I can't remember ever being like anything else. There was a plan up on the screen and it could have been our court.*

Magistrate B: *I came here from [another area] where we had the youth court as a round forum. I thought that was what the youth panel was all about. We always thought it was unusual not to do it that way.*

Magistrate A: *The suggestion that it should be thought of as something new to actually talk to a defendant and to talk to parents! We have always done that. If they had visited our court they would have seen that for themselves. I would seriously like you to record, to register, that there ought to be more 'hands on' feeding into new legislation. I am sure that the powers that be talk to the Magistrates Association, they might talk to the odd chairmen of benches and what have you but they are not necessarily the people who have to deal with young people from day to day, and I think they should come down the scale a little a bit and include one or two of the people at the chalk face.*

Magistrate B: *Not just talking to them but why don't they come and see! You don't get any of the big white chiefs in Whitehall coming out to us. For a while we were all quite offended that we had to go to this conference to be told to do something that we were already doing, goodness knows how many years, and nobody had recognised it! Here we are demonstrating the best practice.*

Magistrate A: *It wasn't just us. Half the conference were up in arms that this was being presented as new.*

Magistrate B: *What does the Lord Chancellor's Department think we are doing! Come and have a look!*

They went on to give examples of the friendly dialogue with which they begin court proceedings. Magistrates have different styles and preferences for engaging young people and their carers. Some will begin by asking about the football club they support, while others will begin by mentioning something to the young person's credit that had been identified in the pre-sentence report.

Nevertheless, there were some dissenting voices against the recommendations for changing the culture of the court. Some doubted whether the way in which young people are addressed makes any difference because 'it is just another adult having a go at them and all they want to know is what you have decided'. One magistrate expressed the view that a setting that looked and sounded too unlike court as it is portrayed on television would not meet expectations and so seem a non-event to the young person and so fail to have an impact. In one court room, in order to seat all parties on the same level, they had tried using only the well of the court, which involved moving all the furniture much closer, but after an incident in which the prosecuting officer had been physically attacked there were concerns for the safety of court personnel and so the furniture was moved back.

As part of the fieldwork for this study the authors sat in on court proceedings in several different youth courts. Even within one county we were aware of contrasts in court cultures, partly determined by the layout and partly by the style of the chair of the bench. But in all of them one striking element which seemed to mitigate against any attempt to relate to young people and their parents was the manner of address used ('Your Worships') and the requirement to stand each time the entrance of the magistrates was announced ('All rise!'). The language and etiquette of the courts imbues the proceedings with a pomposity and theatrical quality which may seem strange or absurd to a generation which has grown up generally free from expectations to show deference or reverence to the adults around them.

CHAPTER 7

Partnership Projects to Tackle the Causes of Crime

Government papers preceding the Crime and Disorder Act 1998 revealed how it was proposed to tackle the 'causes of crime'. The 'framework document' for the Act identified that:

> There is no single or simple way of preventing an individual child or young person offending. The factors that put young people at risk of offending, which are well documented in research, include:
> - troubled home life, including poor parenting, criminal family member, violence or abuse
> - peer group pressure
> - poor attainment at school, truancy and school exclusion
> - personal issues such as drug and alcohol misuse or mental illness
> - deprivation such as poor housing or homelessness.
>
> Tackling these factors, and other specific aspects of a child or young person's offending or re-offending requires input from a range of agencies and services both at a strategic level in planning and resourcing local service provision and at a practical level in deciding and delivering a package of intervention to help prevent offending by an individual child or young person.
>
> (Home Office, 1998, para. 11)

Similarly, the White Paper *No More Excuses* stated that:

> YOTs will deliver community intervention programmes to make youngsters face up to the consequences of their crimes and learn to change the habits and attitudes which lead them into offending and antisocial behaviour. The programmes might adopt techniques such as: group work; one to one work; family group conferencing; and mentoring.
>
> (Home Office, 1997c, para. 8.4)

To help realise these plans, following the Crime and Disorder Act 1998, a sum of £85 million 'development funding' was made available by the Youth Justice Board and local authorities and YOT managers were invited to bid for funding towards the provision of such interventions.

As much as anything else, it was the prospect of developing such interventions that gave staff who were joining the youth offending teams a sense of being part of a new venture which would open up doors for better services. In the preparatory stages leading up the launch of OYOT, there was considerable enthusiasm at the prospect of developing 'state of the art' projects and accessing resources that were previously unavailable. Successful projects already in existence could be further developed and there were prospects of forming new partnerships and accessing services that had previously seemed less attainable. Numerous discussions and meetings took place between the YOT manager and chief officers in the partner agencies in order to plan the development of suitable projects and to identify appropriate experts to co-ordinate and lead them.

It was made a condition of funding by the Youth Justice Board that each project should be evaluated. YOTs were therefore obliged to identify suitable 'local' evaluators as part of the bidding process for development funding. The YJB also appointed teams of 'national' evaluators to co-ordinate the data collection and evaluation arrangements. Each of the evaluation teams focussed on a specific type of intervention, e.g. substance abuse projects; parenting projects. It was intended that they would set the scene for the local evaluations by providing templates for the approach to be taken and the data to be collected. However, the local planning and bidding process was already completed before the national evaluators were appointed, thereby pre-empting opportunities to build in more rigorous evaluation procedures, including uniformity of approach and comparisons groups (Wilcox, 2003).

OYOT's success in bidding for a wide range of projects made it a suitable hunting ground, from an evaluation perspective, for exploring key aspects of setting up projects and for gaining insight into how specialist projects linked with other aspects of YOT service. As we have mentioned previously, this pathway YOT was in the fortunate position of 'inheriting' projects and staff from the multi-agency services previously running in the county - although these had left gaps in provision and some were rudimentary or experimental. There had been a parenting group; a mentoring project; a programme concerned with motor related offences and an arrest referral scheme for young drug abusers. OYOT was awarded funding for ten specialist interventions, some of which built on these previously existing projects and others which were new. This chapter provides an overview of the scope and goals of these projects, and the teething problems and triumphs in setting them up. Examples of good and bad practice emerged as well as ways in which improvements could be made during this early period of development. Many of these have applicability to more than one of the projects and so are considered collectively at the end of the chapter.

Skilled parenting

The reforms gave particular emphasis to the encouragement of responsible parenting, building it into the YJB objectives and introducing new legislation for parenting orders. Many YOTs accordingly, set-up specialist provision in the form of a group programme and/or one-to-one support. The findings from the national evaluation of parenting programmes funded by the YJB were reported in *Positive Parenting* by Ghate and Ramella (2002).

The parenting project in our case-study area was provided by the YOT in partnership with the education service which already had a team focusing on the development of parent education. The project ran a group programme for parents of 10 to 17 year olds who had offended or were at risk of offending, and the parents of young people excluded from school or at risk of school exclusion. Later, eligibility was extended to 'parents who are finding it hard to control their young people and to set boundaries within the home and who are perceived by professionals of being at risk of offending'. As is clear from these eligibility criteria, the project was open to referrals from education welfare officers, schools, courts (via parenting orders) and elsewhere as well as from the YOT. Several facilitators were appointed and trained and the programme was held at several venues in the county, with the location varying according to 'demand' in any one region.

It was a nine-week programme, including the preparatory introductory session, and was structured around identifiable topics such as 'what is adolescence?', 'styles of parenting', 'listening'. Each session used the following structure: *Warm-up* (a game, 'round', relaxation); *Download* (chance to talk about their families, their week and how they are feeling); *Getting in touch* (introducing the main topic for the session with an exercise which puts parents in touch with their own feelings and experiences around that topic); *Video* (a five minute clip from a video provided by the Trust for the Study of Adolescence); *Covering the topic* (builds on the subjects discussed in the video, using discussion, learning methods, role-play); *Planning* (preparation to practice the new skills at home); *Relaxation* (soft music and gentle breathing, soothing words); *Feedback* (parents asked to complete a short feedback form about what they did and didn't like in the session).

The programme aimed to build parents' confidence, self-esteem and knowledge about being an effective parent and to improve relationships within the family, by offering support and providing them with the skills to deal with behaviour problems and conflict situations. The majority of parents who provided feedback at the end of the programme (about a third of them) had indeed increased their confidence in their own abilities to deal with parent-child issues that might arise. It was not a 'miracle cure': most of them continued to experience difficulties with their children, but they had adopted coping skills and strategies that helped them to avert further conflict breakdowns in their relationship with their son or daughter, and they felt empowered by the support from others who were experiencing similar problems.

Comparison of questionnaire ratings completed by 19 participants at the beginning and end of the programmes showed that the percentage of those who felt unable to cope with their child decreased dramatically (from 47 per cent to 5 per cent). By the end of the programme, parents felt better able to understand their child, had fewer arguments and were more able to give appropriate praise. Mothers who returned information at the end of the programme also indicated an improvement in their son or daughter's behaviour. More of them said he or she did as asked (from 32 per cent to 53 per cent) and could be trusted to behave responsibly (from 11 per cent to 32 per cent).

In interviews with parents, they talked about the skills that they had practiced during the group and that had been the most helpful to them. The most basic yet crucial skills of how to listen to and communicate with their son or daughter were frequently mentioned as having led to improvements in their relationships. One mother who, in retrospect, remembered feeling a failure as a mother explained how the programme had helped to release her and her son from a downward spiral of negativity and conflict. Her account provides a vivid example of ways in which the skills of listening, being positive and connecting were consciously applied:

Listening: *Before going on the programme I felt I was like a constant play on this record: You must go to school! You must do this! You have got to do that. At the group they told us about listening and I thought well yeah, but I do listen to him, I don't have a problem with that. But then I came home and he was talking to me and I realised how much I switched off and actually didn't really listen...It takes a lot of concentration to actually listen when you have got things on your mind. I now realise that in the past he has often said to me 'You don't listen to me' and I have thought 'Of course I do'. So I do listen to him more now rather than switching off or not taking in what he is saying.*

Being positive: *The other thing is being positive and I had been negative for so long over school. And so it was about just listening to him talking about his friends and trying to get him to think of things he could do because he wasn't going to school...and to be positive about skills he had got and yeah just seeing him in a more positive light than just this child that isn't going to school. So we talked about some of the things he used to do and could do well. He said he wanted to do more things like take up football and go back to swimming which he'd done a few years ago and given up. He started digging out all his old swimming certificates and it probably made him feel better. So yeah just being more positive helped a lot. Before then, because he wasn't going to school I thought he was a bad child and we shouldn't talk about anything apart from the fact that he wasn't going to school.*

Connecting: *It was thinking of things to talk about. Talking about things that would mean something to him. I suppose it was getting off that whole treadmill of all we talked about was school.*

The feedback from young people whose parents had attended the programme was not nearly so positive but, even so, showed that some improvements had been achieved. Most importantly, a comparison of their questionnaire responses at the start of the programme and at the end of it showed a reduction in the number of offences they had self-reported for the preceding four weeks.

Relevant to the good results reported from programme completers was the skill and commitment of the project leader who developed and co-ordinated this programme, and of the trained facilitators. Also key was the attainment of several conducive venues - mostly 'family centres' - for holding the groups in different locales in the county. Not least, the design and content of the programme was vital in engaging parents and bringing about change.

Unfortunately, quite a few of the parents who were referred often failed to turn up for the first session of the programme that they had agreed to attend. Some parents will always be resistant to attending or engaging with a programme which calls into question their parental competence or requires them to reveal their difficulties to others. The facilitators found that they were able to reduce the numbers of non-starters by arranging a meeting with the parent beforehand to tell them about what the programme involved and to introduce themselves as the person who would be leading the group. This procedure helped to allay apprehensions and to engage the interest of parents.

The completion rate was high once parents had taken that crucial step to attend the first and second session. Not surprisingly perhaps, nearly all of those who attended the programme were female. Only 15 per cent of the total referrals during the period of evaluation were made by YOT practitioners and 90 per cent of these YOT referrals did not complete the programme. It was disappointing that so few parents of young people dealt with by the YOT engaged with and completed the programme. There were various aspects underlying the relatively low rate of referrals and the low rate of 'take-up' by parents who were referred. First, the project was not as visible to YOT staff as was the case with most other projects. Of relevance here, of course, is that fact that those being referred to the parenting projects, unlike referrals to other specialist interventions, were not in a direct and strict sense the 'clients' of the YOT practitioner, unless they were subject to a parenting order. Secondly, YOT officers were not always able to find the time to work with parents to motivate their attendance. Those parents who have the greatest difficulty with their young people may be the most resistant to referral and, when they do attend, the least responsive. YOT officers need appropriate skills to motivate these parents plus sufficient belief in the value of the programme, if they are to help them engage.

Another challenge faced by the project was that of working with parents who are subject to parenting orders. Experience in various YOTs with parenting orders showed that positive outcomes were achieved even when parents were non-voluntary participants (Cusick et al., 2000). The outcomes, in the 'pathway' area, with such non-voluntary participants were mixed. In one group that brought together five parents on parenting orders, their attendance was quite good and it progressed smoothly. But in another group that had a similar number of parents on orders in the attendance was very poor and little was achieved. There were no clear reasons for these differences. A lone parent subject to a parenting order in one group felt unable to talk about it and she held back from participating fully. In contrast, when another group of mainly voluntary participants was informed by one parent that she was on a parenting order it stimulated useful discussion.

Learning points

The task of referring mothers and fathers to a project that, by definition, questioned their competence as parents was not the easiest task for practitioners - especially as parents are not directly the client group of YOT practitioners. Some staff suggested that they have benefited from guidance on how best to broach the subject of attendance at a parenting skills programme. Thus, project staff could usefully provide YOT workers with some training in appropriate techniques to engage the interest of parents in attending. In addition, periodic meetings between practitioners and the project staff to discuss the progress of parents who attend and the progress of their sons and daughters would help to counteract a tendency on both sides to regard the parents as an unrelated client group.

Some parents will always be resistant to attending or engaging with a programme which calls into question their parental competence, yet these are likely to include those with most to learn in developing their parenting skills. The idea of attending such a group and discussing difficulties which are often hidden behind closed doors is likely to be daunting for many. The parenting project was able to minimise this problem by advance home visits to prospective participants once a parent had shown interest.

One of the reasons for under-referral of parents by YOT staff, and under-attendance by those who were referred, was that coping in group settings requires a level of emotional and social stability and social skill. Parents experiencing extreme difficulties in their own lives as well as in controlling and relating to their sons or daughters may simply be unable to cope in a group setting. Project staff and practitioners argued that there was a need for one-to-one provision alongside the group programme. Such one-to-one intervention is also likely to be more suitable for parents made subject to parenting orders who flatly refuse to take part in group discussion or who, if they attend, may diminish it for others. Carrying out such one-to-one work, especially if with parents who may resist the idea that their parenting skills could be improved, requires skills which are additional to those involved in running groups.

The friendship of a mentor

The Audit Commission review *Misspent Youth* commended projects that made use of mentors to give young offenders 'support and encouragement to address their behaviour'. The mentoring scheme used by OYOT had earlier origins and was not a dedicated service for the YOT but took referrals from numerous other partner agencies. It targeted 10 to 17 year olds who were at risk of offending because of negative peer influence, or severe family difficulties, or educational difficulties. To be eligible, the young person had to be open to the idea of having a mentor. There was no shortage of young people who fitted this bill. Indeed, the scheme was open to all in the county but such was the demand on the project, the focus was narrowed to crime 'hot spots' and to prioritising those being 'looked after' in local authority care. Schedule 1 offenders - that is persons convicted of offences against children, as listed in Schedule 1 of the Children and Young Persons Act 1933 - and those with severe mental health problems were excluded as unsuitable for the scheme.

The overall aim of the scheme was to reduce the risk of reoffending by providing opportunities for positive change and personal development. Periodic group activities were organised, such as weekend camping trips, but the essential element of mentoring is a one-to-one voluntary relationship between the young person and an adult mentor, and it was this relationship that was seen as providing the dynamic for change. The scheme defined a mentor as: 'A more experienced adult who is willing to get to know a young person, give time to developing the relationship and share the benefits of their skills, knowledge and life-experience'. It was emphasised that the mentor should act as a role model to the young person. On a basic level of human needs, the scheme provided them with a dependable, supportive relationship: something they might otherwise have lacked. This mentor-mentee relationship gave them an opportunity to be listened to, an awareness of wider choices and different lifestyles, practical advocacy where appropriate and access to constructive leisure pursuits. Mentoring activities ranged from basics, like sharing a take-away and going for a walk, to more planned events such as go-carting and activity-focused residential weekends.

Mentors were motivated by the opportunity to help disadvantaged or troubled young people, but acknowledged gains for themselves in the satisfaction this brought and in useful work experience for related careers. It is a role which clearly calls for careful and monitored recruitment. Publicity to attract suitable volunteers was followed by strict screening, including police, social services and health checks. An analysis of data collected for the evaluation showed that more than 50 per cent of applicants did not end up as active mentors. Those selected were required to attend a 50-hour accredited training course. Out of 200 applicants, 85 completed the training and most of these, at our last count, had taken up the role as a mentor. In common with other mentor projects it was harder to recruit male mentors (Tarling et al., 2001). Two thirds of the mentor applicants had carried out voluntary work before.

Following training, the matching process involved a series of steps. First, one of the supervisors of mentors had an informal meeting with the young person to build up a picture of their interests, their general character and their social circumstances. At the same time, the young person was asked to explain why they would like a mentor. Next, the supervisor and mentoring co-ordinator met in order to 'paper match' the young person with a potential mentor based on the information gathered. The potential mentor was then contacted, provided with relevant information and asked if they were willing to be matched with the young person. If the mentor agreed in principle and if the supervisor was still satisfied with the 'paper match', a three-way meeting was arranged. This meeting - on condition that both young person and mentor were happy to proceed - signified the end of the matching process and the beginning of the mentoring relationship.

Once suitably paired, the mentor was provided with a budget of £35 per month to cover travel and other expenses during weekly meetings and activities with their mentee. Throughout the period of their contact with the young person, mentors were supervised via regular meetings with their supervisor and monthly workshops, and they were provided with administrative support to help with any paperwork. A feature of the scheme which provided additional support and information for mentors was the production of a quarterly newsletter.

The YOT's referrals to the mentoring scheme often had a disappointing outcome. That is, there were 168 referrals during the evaluation period, of which 39 per cent were made by the YOT. Only a third of the YOT referrals resulted in a match with a mentor. This contrasted with 50 per cent of social services referrals who were matched. According to the project staff, the attrition rate for YOT referrals was partly attributed to inappropriate referrals by YOT staff - for example, young people residing outside the targeted areas, or who did not turn up for meetings.

Once the matching was accomplished there was a high chance of the arrangement 'taking off'. Occasionally failures were attributed to the reasons for referring them in the first place: for example, breakdown of family relationships resulting in a move to another area; or a young person succumbing to peer pressure and losing contact with the mentor. Young people who had a mentor invariably voiced enthusiasm for the arrangement. Typical comments were: 'I get on really well with her'; 'It is great to have someone to go places with'; 'I am glad I can have him to talk to'.

The role undertaken by mentors was divided into four main areas: coaching, counselling, facilitating and networking. Through each of these methods, the young person was encouraged and helped to develop skills; to take up constructive leisure pursuits; to make educational progress; and to improve their relationships with friends and adults. Content analysis of interview data helped to identify the essential characteristics of a mentoring relationship that promote positive change. Two dimensions were in evidence: relational and practical. The relational factors were: being non-judgemental, positive reinforcement, dependability and, what amounted to, the fundamentals of counselling such as listening and encouraging. The practical factors were: advice and help in the development of skills and learning, accompanying young people to places, and joint participation in indoor and outdoor leisure pursuits.

An observation made by most mentors and some YOT officers was that, over and above the interesting activities and supportive relationship offered by the mentoring scheme, it was the *voluntary unpaid* nature of the mentor's role that won young people over. When young people found out that their mentor did not gain anything financially for their role, they were stimulated to reinterpret the purpose of the relationship. In most cases, therefore, mentors were able to win the trust and confidence of young people referred to them. Rather than the young person feeling coerced or under pressure to change their behaviour they were able to drop some of their defences and recognise the mentor as genuinely interested in helping them. As one said to her mentor: 'You are not stopping me doing wrong but you are making me think more about it… and I'm not going to do it again'.

YOT practitioners spoke in glowing terms of the benefits for young people who had been matched with a mentor, announcing that, for example, it had resulted in a 'brilliant turnaround with some kids'. Indeed, the idea of providing mentors for young people found universal favour among the YOT practitioners and this scheme was seen to work well, but with one catch: there were not enough mentors to go round. The project became a victim of its own success with the number of referrals far exceeding the number of mentors. Thus YOT practitioners simply stopped making referrals.

Learning points

How frustrating to have such a good project on the doorstep but then to be unable to get at it. Projects that rely on voluntary support are of course vulnerable to fluctuations in the number of people available to take on the role. Also, the mentoring scheme's admittance criteria for young people became increasingly exclusive. While it may seem far better for a YOT to outsource a large scale 'state of the art' project that has the best resources, even though it is not dedicated to YOT clients, experience with this project showed the importance of having a sufficient number of places that are 'ring-fenced' for the YOT.

Another issue illustrated by the mentoring project but applicable to other projects concerns the respective roles taken on by core staff and project staff. It is a feature of the case-management way of working that more of the traditional work of practitioners is farmed out to specialists and to volunteers. Accordingly, mentors who worked with young people referred by the YOT sometimes carried out roles that otherwise were previously the province of practitioners. For example, some mentors attended case conferences with social services, and liaised with education services to get young people back into school or acted as advocates and brokers for the young people in negotiations with other agencies. Also, the specified activities of mentors included counselling - arguably, a professional role that requires, at least, the kind of training undertaken by YOT officers. The appropriateness of using volunteers, who may have attended no more than a few days on a mentoring course, for roles that previously required substantial full-time professional training and were central to statutory services is surely open to question.

Education inclusion

One of the projects that gained development funding from the YJB was labelled 'education inclusion'. This was a difficult project to pin down. 'Education inclusion', like 'restorative justice', was absorbed into practice as an underlying principle but, unlike other specialist projects, there was no single entity to which practitioners could refer young people.

However, there were various procedures, strategies and links to educational initiatives that fell under this heading. For example: procedures for information exchange; protocols for responding to parenting orders; arrangements for reducing truancy and school exclusions; and, co-ordination of arrangements between young offender institutions and schools. A senior education social worker (ESW) was seconded to the YOT to orchestrate all of these elements of the project and to advise YOT staff on educational matters.

The overall objective of these various elements was of course to 'get kids back into school' or to forge routes into further education for those who had left school. The seconded ESW believed passionately that appropriate learning opportunities can make a radical difference to young offenders, steering them away from crime. Indeed words to this effect were made in the mission statement for this somewhat nebulous project. While none of the YOT staff disagreed, some of the former youth justice workers, based on their experience, had a jaundiced view of what would be possible beyond the rhetoric. Despite the new protocols and despite the commitment of the seconded education social worker, the YOT continued to lack an explicit procedure for practitioners to follow in the case of young people not attending school and, therefore, little progress was made.

While under pre-YOT arrangements it was part of the youth justice worker's job to 'turn up at the house of the young person in the morning and escort them to school', under the new system the work became increasingly office-based. Some practitioners admitted that they were out of touch with educational procedures and policy and others suggested that they should be able to make use of the specialist education staff within the YOT rather than spending time themselves in contacting schools. Indeed, some practitioners were disappointed that education staff in the youth offending team were not being more proactive in changing how schools respond and in putting up a defence for children who had been excluded:

We need a really dedicated education worker who is basically jumping up and down on the education department to get things moving.

There is a need for someone out there, gunning for them.

Education inclusion! Who is supposed to be doing that then? I would just say that it is well required. The number of kids who are not attending school! Some of them have been out of school for years and nobody cares really. There is definitely a hole.

Such expressions of dissatisfaction after the YOT had been in operation for some time were perhaps surprising. Apart from the secondment of an ESW manager to oversee the 'education inclusion' project, each of the three YOT units included a practitioner with an education service background, and two of them had a job specification to carry out education-related work. Given these posts, it should have been possible to develop dynamic links between schools and the YOT in working with disaffected or excluded pupils. However, because of the unanticipated volume of work for core staff and, in some cases, because of their own career development choices, these 'education' staff gravitated more towards the generic YOT work and the potential for the development of their specialist roles was forfeited.

Moreover, there was some tension between different perceptions of how school exclusion and truancy should be tackled, although these were not necessarily articulated clearly across the divide. YOT workers argued that schools tend to regard young offenders as 'undeserving' because they are disruptive and unco-operative and bring their school down in the education league tables. Moreover, they may keep troublesome pupils on their records in order to meet targets, but deal with them in such a way as to effectively exclude them. The YOT workers therefore wanted someone to be a champion of the cause of young people who were not going to school. They perceived the education manager to be holding up the education inclusion banner but achieving little of real substance. In turn, the education manager wanted the YOT practitioners to undertake more direct work with young people to motivate their return to school or further education; and he perceived practitioners to be too passive in their support.

In appraising the outcome of the 'education project' there are questions about whether slow progress was due to the project having been poorly conceived in the first place - whether it was ideological rather than being an operational strategy - or whether it did not materialise because, collectively, the education staff appointed lacked sufficient skills and motivation to deliver it properly.

Learning points

From the start, the so-called 'education inclusion' project was a conglomerate of ideas and loosely connected sub-projects. There was no single scheme or process, no project or individual to which young people could be referred. To add to this intangibility there were no staff directly or solely engaged in working with young people who were outside the educational process. Procedures were clarified for parenting orders, given the potential for confusion between educational and youth justice responsibilities. But, apart from this, there was no evidence of an explicit scheme linked to legislation aimed at getting young people into education. With an identified scheme applicable by practitioners, this project would have fared better than it did under the nebulous shape it took, linked to high-sounding but abstract principles.

Therefore, a weakness of this pathway YOT, during the formative period, was its lack of specialist education workers. The role of education workers was never clarified and those who came in with a relevant background for various reasons graduated towards core YOT work. Beyond the protocols and high-level plans for getting children back into school or training provision, there was a lack of clarity about who it was who should be liaising with schools when a young person was not attending. A question remained about whether this should be a specialist role within core practice under a countywide co-ordinator. Any such developments would need to fit in with the education service's own initiatives, such as the placement of ESWs in some schools and links with Connexions. If this is not an area of work that can simply be seen as dealt with 'out there' by the education service, then the YOT remained in need of one or more practitioners with knowledge of the education service who would do some of the legwork in negotiations over individuals who were missing out on education.

Two out of 'three R's'

A basic literacy project set up by OYOT was initially focussed on dyslexia as opposed to literacy difficulties more generally. It was modelled on a probation service project for adult dyslexics and the initial steer was provided by a consultant who was involved in that adult version of the project. Various studies have identified a high proportion of offenders to be dyslexic (Kirk and Reid, 2001). The project was therefore initially intended for young offenders with suspected dyslexia and not already receiving individualised attention. By the end of the YOT's development stage it had evolved into a project that was more broadly concerned with basic literacy skills, despite resistance from some members on the project's steering group who felt it was important to orientate the project towards the specific needs of dyslexics.

A qualified teacher, with experience as a 'special educational needs co-ordinator' and a dyslexia tutor, was appointed to set up and lead the project. Three part-time tutors, also dyslexia specialists, were subsequently appointed on a sessional basis to provide tuition and support to young people. A screening tool was devised which was intended for use by practitioners each time they carried out an assessment using Asset. The YOT practitioner was required to refer to the project any young person who had difficulties in completing the initial screening test: that is, send in the screening results and the young person details. Going on to this next stage though was voluntary on the part of the young person and their parent or carer.

The next stage involved a more thorough assessment using a specialist software package which takes the form of an interactive computer game. This, together with the initial interview carried out by the project co-ordinator, produced a profile of the young person's literacy difficulties. After further discussion and consent, the young person was assigned to one of the tutors, who then arranged an initial meeting with the young person and school staff or the parent or carer.

One of the objectives was to improve participants' access to education, training and employment. Good links were established with schools and, in the case of school age referrals, they were provided with copies of assessment and progress reports. The tutors, who liaised with school staff, kept a record of work done with their tutees and provided monthly feedback to the project co-ordinator about achievements and problems experienced.

The tutoring sessions, by consent, generally took place in school but in some instances were given at the young person's home. The programme of support provided in each case was tailored to the specific needs of the individual depending on what problems were thrown up in the introductory assessment. There was no prescribed limit on the period of support offered.

The tutors were imaginative in the material they used to engage the interest of their young people, responding sensitively to their needs and interests. The following snippets selected from the logs they kept are illustrative:

> *Reading history of Man United and I asked him to write a summary of it. This really caught (young person's) interest.*

> *He was very wound up so we talked and played a game 'All about me': how you feel about life. (Another day) Started reading 'Dracula' - much more of a success! Played a spelling game and looked at an advert and asked questions on it.*

> *Reading 'Livewire Chillers' - he is very enthusiastic about these. Comprehension, puzzle, letter activity. Finished with Boggle. Worked well. Rarely left his seat this week!*

Where possible, the nature of support offered was adapted to accommodate the more pressing problems of the young people referred. The chaotic and difficult lives of some of this client group meant that the support offered could not simply be focused on tuition to meet particular problems with literacy. Tutors were sensitive to difficulties that cropped up for the young people and the need to sometimes delay or interrupt the lesson in order to make time to listen.

> *He worked well but seems quite upset about school and hates coming each day. We read and played a spelling game but I gave him space to talk about himself.*

However, notes of tutors revealed that part or the whole of a session was sometimes spent talking about hard times that the young person was going through. For example:

> *[The young person] was too tired to work as she had been looking after her sister's baby all weekend while her sister was at work. The baby keeps her awake at night too. She looked exhausted.*

> *Mother had taken an overdose in front of him, accusing him of pushing her to do it. Poor little boy! So we had much to talk about.*

Tutors therefore had to balance their specific role with that of supportive adult but without assuming the role of the supervising YOT officer.

Even for those who were able to concentrate fully on the work, dyslexia or illiteracy are difficulties that cannot be resolved overnight. However, measurable improvement can be rapid once support is given. Analysis of questionnaires from tutors and young people who received support indicated that, in most cases, some improvements in literacy and related self-confidence were achieved very quickly. According to the tutors' assessments the majority of young people who had attended for a reasonable period of time had gained in all aspects, especially in reading (79 per cent) and in self-confidence (71 per cent). 'Before' and 'after' questionnaires completed by the young people (with the help of their tutors) revealed improvements in five components addressed by the support: reading; writing; self-confidence; coping strategies; and, expectations about education, training and employment opportunities.

Project staff believed that this intervention decreased offending behaviour by the increasing self-confidence. For some, this occurred when they were told they had dyslexia problems:

> *To know that they are dyslexic and what that means...is for many young people a great boost to their ego, and, for many, that is all they need. So often they have been told they are thick, they are a dummy, or they are always being late for things - all part of the dyslexia problem...One of the first things I do is show them the results of the reasoning test...If I know that they have done well or averagely well then I let them see that result before anything else, then I can say: Just look at this. Did you realise that you were quite bright? They say: No. And I say: Right, now let's see what has been holding you back all these years. And I start picking out the things that have gone wrong for them.*

(Project co-ordinator)

Those who took up the offer of assistance were given general support as well as direct literacy tuition. Support included feedback on what their strengths were and suggested coping strategies to adapt to their difficulties. There were some good results in improving access to education, training and employment, and several examples of major change. Some youngsters started to attend school again after long periods of absence. Others were encouraged and helped to apply for courses at the local college of further education.

In the first 18 months of the project's operation, there were nearly 200 referrals. Almost half of the referrals came from the part of the county where the co-ordinator of the literacy project was based, while the unit of the YOT with the highest caseload made the least referrals. Another noteworthy bias in the referral pattern was that over half were made for young people who were receiving final warnings. This was reassuring, given that this was the first occasion on which young people were assessed; it indicated that any questions about literacy were generally being addressed at the earliest opportunity. However, this was not universal practice: some officers acknowledged that they only screened on rare occasions because of time factors or when literacy problems had emerged in other ways. All officers were well aware that this resource was at their disposal. Eye-catching posters and leaflets about the project were displayed in YOT offices, in courts and elsewhere.

More than 80 per cent of the young people referred took up the opportunity for the further assessment, a surprisingly high proportion given that it was voluntary. This suggests that practitioners were tending to notify the project of 'positive' screenings only if the young person was already indicating a willingness to co-operate. The computer assessment showed that one in ten had less serious literacy problems that could be tackled through self-help or extra parental support. The project co-ordinator explained:

> *With one or two of the older ones, where there have been borderline difficulties which I haven't felt necessitated one-to-one support, I have given them packs of material with games and exercises and some time with me to start them off. If I think that can be done quite well and adequately by the young person and their family themselves there doesn't seem quite the same point in getting involved in a one-to-one once a week. I will give them the option though, if the young person thinks it will be more beneficial.*

Thirty per cent of the referrals from the screening test resulted in the allocation of a tutor. Nearly half of these either did not take-up the first appointment with their tutor or did so but were unco-operative. Those who were unwilling to proceed with a tutor were offered other forms of assistance, such as an information pack for self-tuition or self-referral to other sources of support.

Those at the younger end of the 10 to 17 age-bracket were more likely to start seeing a tutor. Fourteen per cent of the referrals continued to see their tutor beyond four occasions. Over a quarter of these were female - higher than the ratio of female to male young offenders dealt with by the YOT. Attendance by those who agreed to a period of support was often 'hit and miss', but further appointments were always offered following DNAs (did not attend).

Although there was a high rate of attendance for the further assessment to 'diagnose' dyslexia, thereafter the attrition rate was fairly high, with low numbers continuing to see tutors for long enough to receive the support that their difficulties warranted.

It is worth reflecting on possible reasons for this disappointing drop out rate in order to find ways to minimise it. Young people with basic skills difficulties are likely to be ambivalent about receiving help. The process of being investigated and then the potential embarrassment of receiving 'remedial help', even if it is not so labelled, are likely to be psychological barriers. They may also be reluctant to find the time and effort needed to make improvements. The attrition rate could be even higher though if a more stringent criteria for identifying dyslexia is applied. Project staff found that young people and their parents were often relieved and less defensive when their difficulties in reading and writing were attributed to dyslexic tendencies.

Learning points

In setting up this project there was much discussion about definitions of dyslexia and whether a focus on dyslexia was appropriate or too narrow. An assumption was made that very high proportions of offenders do indeed have this problem and that a project geared to addressing it was therefore justified. Equally, it was assumed that those with literacy difficulties for other reasons would be supported by the same means. The screening tool was meant to identify possible dyslexia but was likely to also disclose literacy problems for any other reason. Likewise, even without the screening test, staff were on the look-out for problems that hold young people back and could be expected to refer them because of difficulties that derive from inadequate learning opportunities and insufficient exposure to books and text. YOTs need provision for *all* young people who have difficulties with reading and writing whatever the basis of those problems. The dyslexia label facilitated particular attention to the needs of dyslexics but, as a result, gave the project a narrow identity which was probably unhelpful when attempts were made to gain further funding.

This was another project where the motivation of the young people referred was a pivotal factor, and where it was necessary for staff to draw on an armoury of motivational skills and techniques. Once an initial meeting for further assessment had been achieved, the project co-ordinator used every trick to facilitate interest. One ingenious technique was the use of, in effect, a computer game to assess their difficulties. Another tactic was listing famous people who have been highly successful people but who are dyslexic. Even if some of those referred had difficulties in reading and writing for non-dyslexic reasons, it seems certain that the dyslexia tag made it easier for them to open themselves up to being assessed and to accept support. Paradoxically, this label, which may be more narrowly applicable than is often presumed, seems to have provided a winning formula.

Preparing for employment

A project to help young offenders on the road to employment was one of the most popular with practitioners even though few of them seemed to know what it was called. Alternative names were used, and some simply referred to it by the name of the project worker. The variety of names stemmed from the complex origins of the project, and one of the labels used, *Connexions*, simply reflected the evolution of the project into part of this wider national service which it predated but was later absorbed by.

This education, training and employment (ETE) project started out as a subsection of the *Learning Gateway*, a scheme introduced by the Centre for British Teachers (CfBT) which involved drawing up an individual development plan for unemployed school leavers and then payment of a weekly allowance while they attended various training options. While the *Learning Gateway* was aimed at *all* young people past the statutory school leaving age who needed further training and support to increase their suitability and eligibility for employment, the YOT project was specifically aimed at young *offenders* aged 16 or 17 with such needs. The aim was to provide such young offenders with extra support to improve their access to training and employment and, thereby, to reduce the risk of them re-offending. In an arrangement that was prescient of the national Connexions Service a member of the local careers service was seconded to the YOT to act as a 'personal adviser' to 16 and 17 year old unemployed offenders.

The duration and intensity of contact varied according to need and the willingness of the individual to co-operate. The type of assistance offered ranged from one-off contacts to regular meetings at either the careers centre, YOT office or the young person's home in order to oversee progress and provide continuing support. Practical assistance included helping with the completion of application forms, accompanying young people to job centres and guiding them on how to behave in interviews. In summary, the elements of support that were given included:

• Provision of information.
• Encouragement and motivation.
• Increasing self-awareness of skills and abilities.
• Linking young people into training and job placements.

Reflecting the extent to which young offenders do face employment-related problems, there was a high rate of referral to this project - rather more than it was feasible for one person to deal with in the way intended. During the first 22 months there were 243 referrals. Just a fifth of these were not accepted by the project, either because they were in the wrong age group or because, when checks were made, it was found that they had already been allocated a personal adviser by another careers service. Everyone else referred, was accepted by the project. Twelve per cent of the referrals were female and seven per cent were from ethnic minority backgrounds. Of the 193 who were accepted, 13 per cent failed to attend appointments and 23 per cent who had agreed to be referred subsequently declined help because they had since taken steps to place themselves in work or training. Contact was made with the remaining 64 per cent on at least one occasion.

A third of those who co-operated or stayed in contact with the project found training or jobs for themselves, and a fifth of them were placed in training or jobs by the project. These placements included: work placements (garage mechanics; farm workers; printing trade); and college courses (life skills; child care; carpentry; catering; information technology; GCSEs). While these placements represented the 'hardest' evidence of how the project had helped some youngsters, for others there had been, as one staff member said 'a softer achievement that is more difficult to measure'. That is, they were helped towards employment by guidance, information and practical help. The support given could sometimes be very participatory, as can be seen in the following interview extract:

> *She got me lined up with college and a job and everything. I wrote the letter but she posted it. She got me a lot further than I would have got by myself. I can't stand college and I don't want to go back, stuck in a classroom all day. I have got two application forms I need help with, so I will see her again.*

Providing the young person had not reached the age of 18, cases were kept open so that progress could be monitored and, where necessary, further assistance offered. In interviews with 20 young people who had been referred to the project, they gave mixed information about whether or not it had helped prevent further offending:

> *We have a chat and a coffee and talk about jobs. It is to help me plan my future … Instead of stealing it helps me to see I can do something work-wise for money and not be bored anymore.*

Before I was skiving school and up all night and slept all day. She came up with the idea of college and picked the things I like most. I didn't do GCSEs but I'm making up for it now. She helped me a lot.

With the emergence of the Connexions service the project was integrated into it. The management and running of the project was inevitably affected by these changes. The project worker, following further training, became one of the network of Connexions personal advisers, continuing in a specialist role as adviser to 16 and 17 year olds in the criminal justice system but is also serving as a bridge between Connexions staff and YOT staff for all young people aged 13-17. Because the Connexions service provides every young person with a personal adviser, her role evolved into that of 'gate-keeper' for those who already have contact with a personal adviser elsewhere. The project worker also had a role in sharing knowledge about the criminal justice system with colleagues in the careers service, which facilitated preparatory work for Connexions, including protocols for determining who should be dealing with any young person that is a shared client between the YOT, the YOI and Connexions.

The project was intended to be primarily a one-to-one based service but a groupwork component was also planned for suitable cases. Arrangements for the group programme, however, were shelved, such was the demand for the one-to-one service.

Following the merger, the project worker was still left with a large caseload of young people who were classed as 'hard to reach' and it was decided to drop all plans for a group programme. Priority was given to individual work because it seemed to hold the best chance of engaging and working with young people who were outside mainstream education and had therefore missed opportunities to access further education. The operations manager from Connexions explained that the project worker's role was to:

...think of innovative ways to tune in...get round those barriers which may make it difficult for them to obtain work, and provide intensive support.

The project worker thus needed to be persistent in phoning, writing letters and making home visits. To enhance the accessibility of the project for young people who wished to benefit from it, the project worker arranged sessions and appointments in different branches of the careers service, cutting down on the need for them to make long journeys.

The YOT staff made enthusiastic referrals to the project, comparing it favourably with the career guidance provided before the YOT was set up and describing the personal adviser as 'the right person, in the right job at the right time'. Some disappointment was expressed however in a perceived emphasis on educational and training opportunities when the young people 'want her to find them a job'.

Learning points

Factors contributing to the extensive use of the project were: the commitment and aptitude of the project worker for the role, and the fact that she made herself well-known and clearly visible to practitioners; and the availability of suitable interviewing facilities in careers centres across the county.

However, one person was insufficient to cover the extensive workload involved for the whole county. Plans for a groupwork component lapsed, paradoxically because the extent of one-to-one work left no time to set it up. A group programme, helping young people deal with issues such as whether and how to disclose their offending to prospective employees, would have released more time for individualised support to be given to those most able to benefit from it.

Tackling offending in groups

Groupwork programmes are recognised as an effective way of addressing offending behaviour because it provides a context for young people to challenge and learn from each other (Utting and Vennard, 2000). From the perspective of busy practitioners who are required to provide a specified number of minimum contacts, group meetings maximise the use of time. Accordingly, staff units of OYOT initially set up their own groupwork arrangements on an ad hoc basis, acknowledging that, as much as anything, these were a way of meeting the contact requirements imposed by national standards for youth justice work. Subsequently, a countywide group programme for low risk offenders was developed as well as a cognitive behavioural programme aimed at serious and persistent young offenders - though YJB development funding was only obtained for the latter.

To meet the rising tide of final warnings and performance measures requiring some rehabilitative work, a group programme entitled 'Life Skills' was designed and opened up for countywide YOT referrals after a satisfactory pilot in one of the units. It covered: hobbies and interests; dealing with peer pressure; the implications of a final warning; the consequences of offending behaviour; staying away from crime; and constructive forward planning. All of this was covered in two one-and-a-half hour modules - judged to be sufficient for young people who have only offended on one or two occasions and who are expected to 'grow out of it'.

A more substantial group programme for those requiring more input - an eight-week rolling programme which young people could join at any point - was also developed, aimed at young people on referral orders, 'low tariff' court orders and more serious final warnings. This *Offending Behaviour and Anger Management Programme* was based loosely on a material used locally in the pre-YOT era, and it addressed victim issues as well as subjects evident in its title. The group participants were sometimes 'treated' to a trip to the local young offender institution to give them insight into the consequences of offending. This was a surprising choice of activity in the light of research findings that have associated 'scared straight' programmes with an increase in recidivism compared to control groups (Utting and Vennard, 2000).

Practitioners making use of this group project gave it a vote of confidence and commented on the appropriateness of the group approach for challenging offending behaviour. Positive feedback was also received from some of the participants and their parents, including some parents who phoned up YOT staff to comment on how useful the programmes had been. The groupwork co-ordinator, an experienced youth worker, was well-qualified to run the groups and was considered by staff to have an 'excellent rapport with young people'.

The *pièce de résistance* out of the various group programmes developed in the area was the cognitive behavioural group programme, developed by a clinical psychologist employed by the YOT for this purpose. Careful preparatory research and planning was undertaken so that a high quality groupwork programme for persistent and serious young offenders could be launched. The development of this programme, however, provided an interesting object lesson of how a programme which is *de rigour* can somehow miss the mark - at least initially.

The cognitive behavioural model that was developed for OYOT was a modified version of the McGuire PLUS+ programme developed for the Greater Manchester YOTs. This programme aimed 'to help young people develop their skills for thinking about problems and for solving them in real-life circumstances' (McGuire, 2000: 3) and to apply these skills in order to avoid future offending. The co-ordinator and two members of YOT staff attended an intensive course to prepare them for delivering the programme and to cascade training down to other interested YOT members.

The cognitive-behavioural programme that was subsequently developed required participants to attend 20 sessions (two sessions per week) of group-based activities and structured learning, and was designed for use with up to eight young offenders. It was intended that, before running the group, the project staff and the responsible YOT worker would agree an individualised plan for each young person who would be attending. This individualised plan would then be reviewed half way through and at the end of the programme. A range of evaluation measures were put in place to test for positive change in the young people attending the groups. The evaluation question-naires were set up on *Viewpoint*, an animated computer programme, provided by the Youth Justice Board.

The programme was specifically aimed at serious and persistent young offenders, aged 14 to 17 who were subject to supervision orders, DTOs or ISSPs. Those eligible also included young people with poor thinking skills, but able to work in groups and motivated to change their behaviour. The criteria excluded from the group those who had committed predominantly sexual or violent offences, those who would be too disruptive for the group and those who met the criteria for psychopathy. However, the criteria were intended to serve only as guidelines for referral, leaving some flexibility for each case to be considered on its merit.

In the event, appropriate referrals to this programme were too few and the group could not be run. There were in fact 27 referrals, but these all fell by the wayside for different reasons. In some cases, events overtook them, such as being sent into custody or finding employment. Others received alternative interventions or sentences. Of those who were left, six were considered inappropriate for groupwork. This left two who fitted the eligibility criteria; as this was insufficient to form a group, the co-ordinator provided them with one-to-one cognitive behavioural work.

Practitioners concluded that the eligibility criteria had been 'too selective'. It seems likely, as the co-ordinator suggested, that the *main* reason for low referrals was that the programme was viewed by practitioners as too long and demanding for many of their clients. There was a reluctance to make attendance a condition of an order in case the young person was unable to attend all the sessions. For orders that were already up and running, requiring young people to attend this substantial programme was seen as 'moving the goal posts'. OYOT was therefore faced with the paradox of having a state-of-the-art programme that was not being used and, at the same time, practitioners who identified a 'crying need' for a good cognitive behavioural programme for their clients.

Nevertheless, the preparatory work paid off in the end. A rigorously planned programme was put together and a programme manual was made available for practitioners to follow, together with evaluation tools and rigorous protocols. The Intensive Supervision and Surveillance Programme (ISSP) subsequently provided an obvious client group for the programme for whom the intensity of the programme was ideal. A new member of the mental health team was able to deliver the programme with support from suitably trained practitioners.

Learning points

An extremely thorough and well researched cognitive behavioural programme was set up according to the highest standards, but to the point where it was seen as too exclusive and demanding. There were therefore insufficient programme referrals and it was not possible to run the programme in the first instance. In contrast, less rigorous local innovations had to be fashioned to meet the immediate needs. The introduction of ISSPs subsequently provided a suitable client group for the programme.

Good mental health

There is a high prevalence of mental health difficulties amongst young offenders and this is particularly the case for those who receive custodial sentences (Prison Reform Trust, 2001). The mental health project in OYOT was set up both to assess the mental health care needs of young offenders and to provide treatment or intervention that may improve health, development and quality of life and, thereby, reduce the risk of re-offending. A broad definition of mental health problems was applied, covering healthy emotions and development. The main objectives were: to provide specialist mental health assessments for courts and practitioners; and to liaise with YOT staff and other services to ensure that the mental health problems associated with offending behaviour are addressed. The service was provided by a full-time community psychiatric nurse seconded to the YOT from the Children and Adolescent Mental Health Services (CAMHS), a half-time consultant psychiatrist, and a part-time clinical psychologist. A clinical psychologist who was appointed to run the cognitive behavioural programme was also based with them. Within the YOT, these staff were referred to as 'the mental health team' and this tag became synonymous with the project even though a more appropriate name was proposed.

On the website for the organisation Young Minds, which provides support and information for health workers in YOTs, it is stated that 'front-line workers in the youth justice system need access to specific knowledge and support in order to effectively address the mental health issues that arise in their work'. It was to the credit of the OYOT manager and the project staff that such a mental health service was provided despite minimal financial or other support from the local health sector. Difficulties in gaining contributions and support from health services left the project and its staff feeling particularly insecure. Indeed, one member of the team resigned partly because of this lack of support. A bid to the 'service and financial framework' of the reorganised NHS, to fund a more permanent replacement, was unsuccessful.

Following referrals made by YOT practitioners, the main tasks undertaken by the team were: assessment; consultation and advice; and direct work with young people and their families. The consultant psychiatrist also prepared court reports, often produced as addenda to pre-sentence reports. Various tests and standardised questionnaires were used as aids to assessment and for evaluation purposes. A further task that was taken on by the project was education for YOT officers on mental health aspects of their work. The direct work with young people included treatment directed at specific disorders such as attention deficit hyperactivity disorder (ADHD) and depression, but also dealt with more general emotional and developmental problems seen as relevant to their offending behaviour.

The team adopted a 'multi-systemic approach' whereby mental health issues and offending were analysed in the wider context of family background, educational circumstances, and neighbourhood (Henggeler et al. 1998). While it is standard practice for social workers and youth justice professionals to make holistic assessments of offending behaviour and to work 'multi-systemically' - albeit not under this label - clinical psychology and psychiatry are traditionally more detached. One of the 'clinicians' (as they sometimes described themselves) explained the value of the model they were applying:

Working multi-systemically makes it a lot easier to integrate the mental health and offending behaviour, because it is in the bigger system that the offending behaviour starts and is being maintained. And looking at it multi-systematically gives us a very good understanding of how this has come about and an understanding of where we fit in, what is the bit that we can do about it. If you are focused on say depression or anxiety, it is not always easy to understand how they are related to offending. But of course the bigger the lens and the bigger the system you are understanding, the easier it is to see how all these things actually are interlinked. So it is really helpful to sit on the two chairs at the same time.

The team found that in-depth therapeutic work, focused on mental health problems, was often not realistic because of the range of problems in some families. In such cases, even when a clear psychological disorder was diagnosed, the task was to identify, with the YOT practitioner, which other problems needed to be tackled first.

Other features of the team's modus operandi were home-based work, working in pairs, and co-working with YOT officers. The practice of working with young people in their homes was partly a response to the high percentage of missed appointments that had been arranged at YOT offices and other venues. Home visiting was also a response to a shortage of appropriate interviewing rooms.

Much of the mental health team's direct work with young people and their families was done in pairs, generally with another member of their own team but sometimes with a YOT practitioner to whom the young person was already known and who would therefore facilitate contact. To some extent though - and in contrast to standard youth justice practice - co-working was arranged for safety and support when home-visiting:

We started to realise that we really have to work in pairs because often the family is so aggressive and feel that they have been treated very badly by other agencies like schools or social services. So there is a lot of resistance and you need a lot of time with them to make them feel that they can actually trust you and that you are serious about helping and supporting them.

Even though home-visiting proved to be challenging because of the need to compete for attention with television, phones, dogs and cats, it was useful in gaining a sense of what 'life was like' for that young person. A problematic aspect of the family based approach and home visiting was that the mental health workers were likely to encounter problems that were the responsibilities of other agencies, particularly social services, but which were increasingly being dealt with by the YOT.

Available records showed there were 99 formal referrals to the mental health team during the 18-month evaluation period. Of these, 83 per cent were male and 10 per cent were from ethnic minority backgrounds. Direct work was carried out by a member of the mental health team with 50 per cent of the referrals. In 40 out of 50 cases the young person engaged with the intervention and, in another five, work was done with the family even though the young person refused contact. Direct work was attempted with another ten per cent who did not engage. In over a quarter of the cases, input from the project was in the form of assessment, discussion and advice, including court reports in some cases. There were seven cases where another mental health service was already involved.

In a third of the cases the team completed Health of the Nation Outcome Scales for Children and Adolescents (HoNOSCA rating scales) at the start of contact and again after a period of intervention. This small data set showed consistent improvement along mental health and behavioural dimensions according to the assessments of the project staff.

Practitioners, on the whole, viewed the mental health project as an invaluable supplement to their work with young offenders. It had resulted in quicker access to mental health assessment when previously there would have been long delays. When young people were referred they were usually seen within two to four weeks. This compares with an average wait of four months for mental health assessment through other channels. The other positive outcome of the project was greater success in gaining the co-operation of young people who were resistant to receiving treatment. Because the project was situated 'outside' of the usual medical setting, and because YOT practitioners had acted as 'go-betweens', it was possible to gain the trust of marginalised or defensive young people who would otherwise steer clear of mental health interventions.

For the project staff the young offenders who were referred, with a few exceptions, constituted a challenging 'client group'. They contrasted with 'patients' who identify themselves as in need of help with mental health issues and seek it out. Motivation of the young person and their carer is critical and in-depth therapeutic work was possible in only a small percentage of cases where the family encouraged the intervention and the young person was willing to co-operate.

Unkept appointments were a theme of the work however. Young people were sometimes referred to as DNAs (did not attend). Apart from the barriers of low motivation and chaotic family situations, the multifaceted nature of their problems made it difficult to carry out focussed mental health work. Many of the young people referred did not have psychiatric problems; rather they were psychologically and emotionally troubled. The nature of the work carried out by the team therefore varied, as one of the team explained, 'along a continuum from, on one end, a totally chaotic situation to a more structured situation on the other end that allows individual work to be done'.

The mental health team emphasised the value of good communication and liaison between themselves and YOT practitioners. They saw themselves as working alongside each other as cases progressed. One of the team gave this description of their inter-agency work:

> *Probably the most valuable aspect of my work is about being available to YOT officers, them knowing they can ring us up and talk through cases, and think about things with us, and that we are available to them to help out with a particular thing that helps them move on so they don't feel stuck. I think it is a sort of organic process. We are almost in constant contact. I will contact the YOT officer after I have seen their young person and give feedback, or if they DNA I usually go and see a YOT officer and discuss what's best to do next so it is like we are together all the time. It is almost not feedback but working together.*

From its difficult beginnings without office space, this project developed into being a true example of 'joined-up' work. Easy access between the YOT units and the mental health project facilitated the provision of a seamless service. Although the mental health team was a countywide resource, the experience of co-working with officers was carried out partly on a geographic basis so that local knowledge about facilities could be developed.

Learning points

The way in which this project developed gave rise to questions about how responsibilities should be divided between, first, the mental health team and YOT practitioners and, second, between the mental health team and other agencies. Mental health clinicians made a practice of home visiting and thus got caught up in family-based work that had previously been the province of the social services. This was an example of how inter-agency work - and the diffusion of roles - can result in practitioners becoming more holistic in their approach while, at the same time, there is a danger that they cross the line and end up carrying out someone else's job as well as their own.

That is, they believed that social work colleagues saw them as appropriately taking on such responsibilities by virtue of their role in the YOT and so needed to reassert their specialist mental health roles. Similarly, when home-visiting, they sometimes dealt with diverse problems that are the province of YOT workers but for which there is now less time because of case management roles. While home visiting may well be 'good practice' from the point of view of mental health provision, it was not appropriate for them to fill a vacuum resulting from the switch from casework to case-management.

This project exemplified partnership tensions on a top management level even though the inter-agency work between health service specialists and YOT workers was often excellent. The YOT was seen by the local department of child and adolescent psychology (DCAP) as a source of competition for funding. When the project staff were stuck for places to interview young people referred by the YOT, they were not allowed access to interview rooms in the relevant hospital. A more co-operative arrangement would have been apt given that the mental health team took over some of the young people who would have come into the ambit of DCAP.

The division of responsibility between the mental health project and other mental health services was unclear. Some of the young people seen by the team were in need of long-term support beyond the span of time when they might be dealt with by the YOT. CAMHS sometimes referred young people who were not known offenders but who were self-reporting offending or seen as at risk of offending. There was a need, therefore, for clarification about which young people at risk of offending should be seen by the YOT's mental health team and which by CAMHS. A scenario can be envisaged where both services would end up 'swapping' clients in an effort to keep their own workload down.

Making amends

Providing reparation activities for young offenders is a major undertaking requiring extensive involvement of members of the public. An ambitious reparation scheme was successfully set up in OYOT. The scheme was well documented and rigorous protocols and procedures were put into place. It has featured in Youth Justice Board publicity as an example of good progress in youth justice reforms (YJB, 2001c). Despite a delayed start, extensive progress was quickly made under the leadership of a creative and dedicated co-ordinator and it developed into a large-scale enterprise. Around 30 sessional workers were employed as reparation supervisors and subsequently a wide range of community reparation was made available countywide.

Young people were referred to the scheme as a result of court orders requiring set hours of reparation to be achieved. Reparation can form an integral part of several court orders, but it was referral orders which placed the greatest demand on the scheme. Over three quarters (78 per cent) of young people referred to the scheme were subject to a referral order.

The reparation project enabled young people to repair the harm that was caused through their crime, whether via direct or indirect reparation. Direct reparation was achieved either in practical and tangible ways (such as financial compensation or repairing the damage done to property) or through symbolic measures (such as a letter of apology or an explanation to the victim). Where the ideal of direct reparation was not possible - because there was no identified victim or because the victim refused - the scheme followed a principle of finding projects that were in some sense 'restorative'. For example, the chosen project had some bearing on the offence that had been committed - such as cleaning graffiti in a public place if the offence had involved damage to someone's property. Reparation projects were also carefully matched to the young person's age and abilities.

For each young person referred, the co-ordinator appointed a sessional worker to be the supervisor. The supervisor then visited the reparation site and conducted a health and safety risk assessment. Where parental consent was required, the reparation supervisor met with the young person's parents or carers. The reparation then commenced and, if necessary, transport was provided for the young person. The supervisor kept a diary of events and reported any contacts or missed appointments to the YOT officer.

A full training programme was set up for the sessional staff who acted as reparation supervisors. It covered: restorative principles and risk factors; victim awareness; motivational interviewing techniques; an outline of the scheme's protocols; and training in health and safety risk assessment. They also received a one-day 'first aid in the workplace' training course. Ongoing training was provided in the form of one-to-one and group supervision.

A team of supervisors with a diverse range of skills made it possible to meet requirements and to organise an extensive range of activities. These ranged from painting a mural in a youth club to repairing prosthetic limbs for land-mine victims. The most successful placements were those that were the least complicated to set up and run, and those where supervisors were able to form a meaningful relationship with the young person.

Most (87 per cent) of the young people referred to the project started reparation activities, and out of the 158 'starters', a remarkable 96 per cent successfully completed their reparation. Such a high rate of completion seems indicative of the quality of the projects and high standard of project staff.

Evaluation forms completed by reparation supervisors were returned for 75 cases. Average ratings on a scale of one to five (where 1 = strongly agree and 5 = strongly disagree) showed that young people engaged well with the activity and the placement (average rating of 1.6) and the placement was appropriate to the young person's skills (1.8). However, the placement was less often thought to be clearly relevant to the crime (3.3). Out of 28 young people's questionnaires returned to the evaluators, 26 young people reported that they understood better the effect of their behaviour on others, 27 reported that they had been held responsible for their behaviour and 25 said they were treated with respect and dignity and had been well prepared for the reparation process.

Staff and supervisors on the project who were interviewed stressed that reparation benefited the community and was a constructive way of dealing with offending. Some commented that when young offenders are seen participating in reparative activities in the community, this helps alter perceptions that most young people are 'vicious hoodlums'. Overall, the staff felt that young people in general had been co-operative and had seen their reparation activities as appropriate and valuable. Staff also identified reparation as a penalty that made sense to young people because they perceived it as constructive for others as well as an opportunity to develop new skills for themselves. While reconviction data were unavailable, all project staff provided examples of young people who they believed had been influenced to desist from crime because of their reparation experience.

Practitioners praised the reparation project as a 'positive experience for kids' but noted that there was scope for much more direct reparation of clear benefit to victims. The project staff were keen to increase opportunities for direct reparation and to make use of the YOT's victim liaison scheme in order to increase victim involvement. In the meantime, they attempted to find projects that took account of the victim's wishes. In most cases where a direct meeting was inappropriate, victims were given the opportunity to suggest the community reparation they would like to take place and were provided with feedback at the end of each placement. In addition, indirect or 'shuttle' mediation took place in some cases whereby information was passed from victim to offender via the co-ordinator, helping the young person to appreciate the victim's perspective.

Even where projects are not specifically for victims, nor linked to the crimes committed, the mere fact of doing something constructive in the community can promote a sense of community consciousness. One reparation supervisor made this point in the first newsletter for the project:

> *At first I had reservations that creative arts projects may not be at all relevant to the crimes committed or the youths themselves and the skills they might wish to develop. However, over the course of the past few months I have become convinced that the work we have done is a valid way of encouraging social awareness and self-reflection.*

The scheme coped with a large volume of referrals and, unlike other projects, it was unable to be selective because the scheme was part and parcel of court orders. To meet this demand additional staff had to be recruited. One of the difficulties encountered by project staff was that young people did not always turn up to their reparation placement. This was particularly frustrating for reparation supervisors who put enormous effort into setting up a placement and liaised with various community members. Unfairly enough, when a young person failed to keep a reparation appointment, the supervisor did not receive due payment.

Learning points

Opportunities for direct reparation rarely occurred. Nevertheless the project could still be categorised as an example of 'restorative justice' because the projects were cleverly designed to benefit others in the community and, where possible, to take account of victims' wishes.

The project was not linked up to the final warning scheme. Only one of the referrals for reparation during the evaluation period followed a final warning, while the reparation project was most typically used for referral orders. Given that the concept of joined-up practice is central to youth offending services, it was surprising to find that all the reparative and restorative justice elements of the YOT's work were not better co-ordinated. However, by the end of the evaluation there were plans to establish an inter-agency 'restorative justice service' that would unite the relevant work of the YOT, the police service and other agencies. This was expected to improve the detailed planning of work with and on behalf of victims and to expand the scope for direct reparation.

Responsible driving

Most of the interventions to tackle offending are not ones which young people would eagerly subscribe to, at least not without coaxing. Motor projects are among the exceptions in that they may appeal to an interest or leisure pursuit. The attractions of driving as a skill and the 'grown up', machismo qualities of motor projects give them kudos. The motor project used by OYOT had the added attraction of being one which had been well publicised. Indeed Trax, a local company with charitable status, had been visited during its short history by several very famous people including royalty, prime ministers and home secretaries.

The company ran similar programmes for non-offenders but the YJB development funding enabled it to reserve one group for referrals from the YOT. This was the *Responsible Road Users Programme*. In addition to the main programme run at the headquarters, shorter courses during the school holidays were provided in a mobile unit located in the north and south of the county during school holidays. The main programme consisted of a seven week 'rolling' course and participants met weekly for a two-hour session, half of which was spent in a motor mechanics workshop. The group was led by two members of staff, a youth worker with expertise in motoring offences and driving law, and a mechanic who also ran the workshop. Half of the time was spent in the workshop dismantling and reassembling go-carts. The specified aim of the programme was to prevent and reduce offending by 13 to 17 year olds with a history of offending, especially motor-related offending. Specific objectives were:

- To provide information to encourage responsible road use.
- To challenge the attitudes associated with their offending and irresponsible motoring activity.

Virtually all those referred had committed motor-related offences although the main charge at the time of YOT involvement may have been another type of offence. The group programme, not surprisingly, was mainly about legal and safety aspects of driving, but it covered other topics, including sexual health and careers advice. There was even an opportunity to develop IT skills while preparing a curriculum vitae.

Unlike some of the other specialist provision for the YOT, project related delays seldom occurred and there were no waiting lists. The use of a rolling programme made it possible for young people to commence the programme on the same day as their initial interview by project staff. Other good features of the programme were that it was held in spacious and well-equipped premises, decorated with appropriate posters, and the milieu was friendly and informal. For young people interested in motor vehicles, the setting was ideal.

The work of this company with young people generally was reputed to be of a high standard and effective. The results obtained with YOT-referred young offenders during the evaluation were somewhat disappointing. Questionnaires to test knowledge were filled in by the young people at the start and at the end of the programme (by those who were still around) allowing some indication of what had been learned. The scores showed that most participants on the programme increased their knowledge of the legal aspects of driving but their attitudes to safety on the roads, if anything, deteriorated. These findings were based on small numbers because of low numbers completing the programme. Interviews with young people who had attended did not inspire great confidence in the programme's effectiveness. Half of them reported that they had committed further offences.

There were 80 referrals by YOT staff to this programme during the evaluation interval; less than had been anticipated. It was disappointing therefore that a relatively high proportion (30 per cent) did not even get to the initial interview. On some occasions only one young person turned up for the programme. Staff identified various reasons for low referral and low attendance, some more plausible than others. It was suggested that:

1. The programme was held in the wrong place. However, the programme was held in premises within reasonable distance of the bus and train station, and there was alternative provision in a mobile unit for those who lived too far away from the main programme.
2. The programme was held during school hours. Initially the programme was held in the afternoon and attendance improved when it was switched to an early evening time. After that, though, an alternative objection was that it was not a safe place for young people to access on dark autumnal and winter evenings, being set in an industrial estate.
3. The rules of attendance were too rigid. If a young person missed more than two sessions in sequence they were required to start the programme again. YOT workers thought there should be some relaxing of these rules to accommodate disorganised lifestyles of young people.
4. Not enough suitable cases to refer. The number of young offenders committing motor-related offences had dropped. Young offenders who would have been suitable had already attended a similar programme as part of a diversion programme before the YOT was formed.

Forty four per cent of those who made it to the initial interview were 'completers'; that is, they attended from six to eight sessions. Reasons which the young people gave for dropping-out often related to the person rather then the project: illness; family crisis; further court appearances. Reasons relating to the project were location, time held and disappointment that the mechanics session involved go-carts rather than cars.

It was not welcomed as vociferously by YOT staff as some of the other YJB-funded projects. Project staff were disappointed by the level of interest shown by YOT practitioners and poor responsiveness and feedback to communications. The YOT staff enjoyed more direct contact with staff linked to some other projects and, in contrast, the motor-project may have suffered from being 'out of sight, out of mind'. Efforts to promote the programme more, including a presentation to staff at one of their away days, were followed by increased referrals and attendance.

Learning points

The strengths of this project were also its weaknesses - and the learning points have relevance to other specialist groupwork programmes.

The advantage of a rolling programme is that young people can join the group immediately without going on a waiting list but the 'trade off' is that it can be difficult to establish any sense of being part of a group when the membership is constantly changing. To compensate for this, efforts should be made to provide a sense of structure and continuity for each person attending and to help the group gel on each occasion.

The programme was held in a comfortable and spacious venue which was well-equipped and displayed various relevant posters and information. The group was led in a relatively relaxed, informal manner, adapted to the needs and responsiveness of those attending. This made it a particularly unthreatening and 'user friendly' group. However, an informal atmosphere can affect programme integrity.

The breadth of the programme and the openness of the referral criteria carried a mixed message about the content of the programme. Its identity as a programme about motoring behaviour was diluted by attention to other issues affecting young people. Results for such a programme may be better if it is more exclusively about driving-related behaviour.

The project made use of an in-built monitoring and evaluation package, allowing comparative measures at the start and at the end of the programme. It would be more useful in practice if those who 'drop out' or do not attend the final session could be persuaded to complete the final questionnaires. A substantial section of the evaluation questionnaires could not be used for the present group because the majority were under 17, i.e. not old enough for a full driving licence. The specific outcomes for those who do complete the final evaluation should be shared with the young people and those with responsibility for them.

Records were kept by the group leader of each young person's progress on a weekly basis. There was the potential for better information exchange between the project and the responsible YOT officer. Information on referral forms was not always sufficient and, ideally, should have been supplemented by discussion.

Tackling drug abuse

A partnership formed by the YOT with a service for substance misusers showed some of the problems that can arise in partnerships between local authority services and the voluntary sector. A drugs worker was seconded from an agency in the voluntary sector to the city office of the YOT with a view to providing a countywide resource for drug users referred by the YOT. The voluntary agency specialised in working with substance misusers, of all ages, at critical points in the criminal justice process, notably arrest, to engage people's motivation at such times of crisis.

The seconded drugs worker had previously been the key worker for an arrest referral project that contacted young drug abusers who had been arrested with the aim of providing them with advice and support. The partnership with the YOT was a development from, and modification of, this prior project though it was not dedicated to arrest referral services. Rather, a range of services was offered, including assessment of drug use, provision of drug-related information, counselling and a treatment plan, and referral to other services to deal with related problems.

This proved a very demanding role for one person covering the whole county, given the extent of minor drug use by young people and the geographic area covered. Given the high level of demand, it became necessary to narrow the availability of the service down to what were described as '*problem* drug users'; that is, high risk drug users, particularly those who were injecting. Although technically the 'substance abuse' specialism included provision for alcohol abuse, in practice the focus was on drug abuse only.

The project did not develop well. There were emerging differences in the 'agendas' of both agencies. An aspiration for this voluntary service in joining the YOT was to draw attention to the lack of services in the county for drug misusers under age 18 and they had envisaged the partnership as a 'springboard' to more resources. In planning the partnership, they had anticipated funding for at least two members of staff, but the acquired funding meant that plans had to be scaled down. From the perspective of the YOT, some staff were disappointed that the drugs worker was not available to support and advise less serious drug abusers - although those with clients who were high risk abusers were satisfied with the service.

The project also ran into practical problems. The drugs worker found that being based in one unit of the YOT was impractical given the peripatetic nature of the work. Another practical difficulty arose from the agency's stance on the confidential nature of its services to clients. Practitioners therefore lacked feedback to inform their subsequent work with the young people referred to the drugs worker. Similarly, the evaluators were not given access to basic details needed to evaluate the work being carried out.

In the face of such difficulties, commitment to the partnership faded on both sides threatening the continuation of the project. There were other, more serious, impediments to the continuation of the project. The YOT managers experienced an increasing lack of co-operation from the project worker. More fundamentally, as revealed in discussions with the evaluators, the YOT's goal of preventing and reducing offending was not shared by project staff. Not surprisingly, the contract for continuing the partnership was not renewed.

In summary, the factors that led to this failure, as outlined above, were:
1. The voluntary agency was disappointed with the size of the grant and had to compromise on the proposal they had drafted.
2. The terms of the secondment and the size of the workload were perceived to be impracticable by the seconded worker.
3. The YOT staff valued the work that was done under the contract but were disappointed by the restriction of the service to more serious drug abusers.
4. Relations deteriorated and co-operation with YOT managers and YOT goals was withdrawn.

Fortunately, the demise of this partnership for drug specialist work coincided with new options for the provision of drug services in YOTs. Subsequently, two full-time and one part-time substance misuse workers, based in community primary care teams, were appointed to work with young offenders as part of the Drug and Alcohol Action Team (DAAT) strategy. Before these new options materialised however, the breakdown of the partnership led to a hiatus in the availability of a drug abuse service dedicated to the YOT.

Learning points

Perhaps the main lesson to be taken from the failure of this contract is the obvious one that, for a partnership to work, the details of the contract need to be properly understood and agreed and both parties need to be sure that the arrangement is going to be mutually satisfactory before proceeding.

Working with young sex abusers

Another important service 'bought into' by the YOT, provided specialist work with 10 to 17 year olds who have engaged in sexually abusive behaviour. This service was a pre-existing unit of the social services department which had been somewhat neglected as a result of staffing problems and inadequate resources. Funding from the YOT and a new appointment to lead the project were helpful in its regeneration. The unit provided case conferences, risk assessments and court reports and, where appropriate, programmes of intervention with young sex abusers and their parents or carers. While some of the young people were referred following conviction for a sexual offence, more often the referrals were made because a sexual offence had come to light although there had been no court proceedings.

The intervention programme, usually provided with a co-worker, followed a structured cognitive behavioural model. It aimed to assist the young person in controlling their sexually abusive behaviour and to provide parents or carers with guidance to help them identify any future risk and to use external controls to manage that risk. The duration of the programme was variable to fit the needs of the individual case.

During the evaluation period, about two to one of the referrals were made by social services rather than the YOT, reflecting a tendency for sexual abuse cases involving child victims not to result in court proceedings. In the project leader's view, all the referrals had been appropriate but, based on surveys of the extent of such abuse, it was possible that other appropriate cases had not been referred because of the hidden nature of such behaviour. The project manager suggested that, with training on what to look out for, YOT staff could be more proactive in identifying potential sexual abuse so that preventative steps could be undertaken.

Although the number of referrals from the YOT was low, the project was restricted in the amount of work it could undertake because of under-staffing. For a period the project manager worked solo without even administrative support. The staffing situation had gradually improved and, at the last check, the project manager and a full-time social worker were anticipating an additional member of staff.

Young people with psychiatric problems were not accepted for the programme of intervention. It was planned that the mental health team would screen all young sex abusers to ensure that if any did have mental health problems they did not slip through the net and alternative interventions could be put in place. It was important to distinguish serious psychiatric problems that may underlie sexually abusive conduct from attempts to excuse abusive behaviour and to shift responsibility for it onto mental illness. These arrangements to co-ordinate work were not always carried out and there was scope for better linkage between the two projects, and for liaison with sex offender projects for adults.

The majority of YOT officers did not make referrals to this project and so were unable to comment on the quality of the service. A critical feature for those who did was the desirability of co-working with the specialist staff of the sex-abuser project. Arrangements did not always go well: the project staff questioned the ability of some YOT staff to carry out this role. They advised that staff at each unit should be selected and trained as adolescent sex offender specialists who would then co-work with project staff.

The project manager suggested that the referrals received could be as few as 50 per cent of the actual picture and that training for an early warning system should be put in place. There was a need for an established referral criteria and a systematic referral process. The project also needed further specialist support so that integrated evaluation of outcomes using psychometric testing could be carried out.

Learning points

A concern, in relation to this project, was that very few referrals were made and it was possible that some appropriate cases which had not come to light through court proceedings had been missed. Training should be provided so that YOT staff can be more proactive in identifying potential sexual abuse in order for preventative steps to be undertaken. As with the mental health project, there was a need for the expertise of a forensic psychologist to carry out psychometric testing in order for the programme outcomes to be suitably evaluated.

Throwing out a safety net

For a period, the YOT also subscribed to a specialist team which worked with people who have multiple problems and who do not readily fit into the categories for which support services exist. That is, because of their behaviour they would be barred from other services, or they would fail the selection criteria because of the multi-dimensional nature of their problems. This 'safety net' service therefore typically dealt with people who had a combination of such problems including one or more of the following: learning difficulties; poor mental health; offending behaviour; substance misuse; accommodation difficulties; chaotic or bizarre behaviour; risk of self-harm. It was also an 'outreach service' for people sleeping rough. One of the strengths that the service publicised was that, unlike statutory services, they had the 'flexibility and persistence to open doors which have previously seemed firmly closed'. Thus this team worked with individuals who had a history of refusing other forms of help. They were persistent in efforts to engage the client and to put them in touch with the services that they needed (Dewhurst, 2000).

The safety net service was set up with a grant from the Department of Health and Social Security and was later jointly funded by local authority services and several charities. The partnership with the YOT arose when the project was considering the possibility of extending their service to a younger age group. Discussions took place with the first YOT Manager about the feasibility of referrals from the YOT of 16 and 17 year olds who might fit into the miscellaneous, misfit categories targeted by the model. In previous years the project had worked with small numbers of young people in this age group, therefore it was reasonable to anticipate that there would be referrals from the YOT. A contract was accordingly set up.

However, hardly any referrals were made, although some additional preventative work was done with 16 and 17 year olds referred by other services. An explanation given by YOT staff for the low number of referrals was that children who could have been referred were already the statutory responsibility of another agency, usually social services. According to the safety net project, however, there was a misperception that it existed only as an 'outreach' service and therefore was only appropriate for young people who did not have a statutory worker. Another factor underlying low referrals was that some YOT practitioners had associated the service with accommodation issues and homelessness and had not used the service because their recent caseload did not include anyone living rough.

In an effort to boost referrals and provide the YOT with value for money, a link-worker from the safety net team was identified to liaise with the YOT and to raise the profile of the project. When the level of referrals continued to be low, a decision was made to expand the partnership to include parents and relatives of YOT clients, if these parents or relatives fitted the profile of someone with multiple problems and falling through the health and social services net. The idea was that the specialist team would provide complementary support to the work of the YOT in cases where the young person might be offending because of their family circumstances. Despite adapting the partnership arrangements in this way, this continued to be a project that was not used by the YOT.

Why was this otherwise busy outreach and fall-back service underused by YOT staff? At the start of the partnership an assumption was made that the formation of the YOT would result in more, not less, referrals of young people in this age group, because 'a new mainstream service tends to uncover more potential work'. The director of the project proposed several reasons for the surprising outcome:

- YOT practitioners are unlikely to perceive young people in their caseloads as fitting the problem profile of people normally dealt with by this service, because at that age, however bad their problems, they would likely be perceived as transitional rather than as chronic.
- The offer of voluntary counselling and support is less likely to appeal to a 16 or 17 year old than someone older.
- Most obviously, the intensive work offered by the outreach service was not dissimilar to work being done by YOT officers themselves, faced with clients who have a range of problems. Whereas other projects may be seen as supplementing the key worker role and something they could not provide themselves, a referral to this outreach team would be like handing on the work that they were doing themselves.

In the end, the low referral of young people was taken to be a good sign that the needs of 'hard to place' young people were being met and that the mesh of services provided by the multi-agency YOT was fine enough to catch them.

Learning points

This contract provided the YOT with a clear link to a service for the most troubled young people that, importantly, would still have been there for them beyond the age of 17 when they no longer had the YOT to fall back on. The service was not used and therefore the contract had not provided the YOT with value for money. Questions therefore had to be asked. Was this because the service was unneeded or was it because the service had not been appropriately promoted? While perhaps the contract had over estimated how much the service would be needed for children and young people on YOT caseloads, on the YOT's side there was probably underuse of the extended service offered to work with problem parents. YOT officers rarely had time to work with parents whose chronic problems were contributing to the offending related problems of their clients, and so the underuse of the outreach service for this purpose was a missed opportunity.

Projects: the bigger picture

The development of projects available to a youth justice system, like the development of YOTs themselves, was like the turning of a kaleidoscope in which formations kept rearranging themselves and taking on new shapes. Some specific projects became more general (e.g. the project for dyslexia which only dealt with other literacy problems by default, became a project for literacy problems more generally). Some small projects were later subsumed by larger projects (for example the project helping to prepare young people for employment was subsumed by the national Connexions scheme) and some took over parallel projects outside the YOT (e.g. the YOT eventually took control of the wider restorative justice initiatives in the Thames Valley Police Service for young people under 18 years of age). Other shifts in character were related to staffing. Specialist staff seconded from other agencies came to the end of their contract and their specialist role was taken on by 'core' YOT staff, or specialist sessional staff who helped to run group programmes were replaced by YOT staff who had a particular interest in co-leading a group together (for example, the parenting group or the cognitive behavioural programme). Once projects had been developed and were ready to go, the replacement of some expensive specialist staff by YOT staff was cost saving and also gave back to YOT staff some of the more direct work with clients that they had partly lost.

The anticipation that YOT staff had, when YOTs started out, of easier access to a wider array of specialist projects and resources gave way to some disillusion. YOT staff increasingly felt that the projects were not quite right for their clients and that they were referring young people to the next best thing. Projects were seen as having their own agenda and YOT staff felt they were having to accept what was on offer and hope for the best. Some looked back on previous practice and concluded that they had been better off in the past:

Although we didn't have these projects available we came up with more of a plan of what the young person needed and then dug around to try to identify that from different places. What happens now is that we ask ourselves 'Well how can we slot them into what's available?' whereas previously we would be more imaginative. I can think in the past of coming up with quite creative things like specified activities programmes and constructive use of their leisure time and things for young people attached to their supervision orders to keep them out of custody. Whereas now it just wouldn't happen in that way - you just make do with what's there.

(Former youth justice worker)

General learning points

Some learning points for specific projects have already been identified. Other findings have a wider relevance for good practice in developing and utilising interventions to address offending related needs.

A critical distinction to be made is between projects that are 'YOT-dedicated' developments targeting only YOT clients and 'multi-user' projects in the wider domain that take referrals from various agencies. Clearly, there is a 'trade-off' between the advantages and disadvantages of each, as examples described in this chapter have shown. Buying into a larger, multi-user project, perhaps already in existence, augurs a well resourced intervention provided by experts. However, such a project is not tailored to YOT clients and may be therefore less than ideal. Where a specialist project is not exclusively for the YOT there is a risk that its resources and energies are increasingly directed away from catering for YOT referrals and towards more motivated non-YOT referrals, thereby decreasing its accessibility to the YOT. This is particularly likely if the referrals from the YOT are low or if the drop-outs are high. For example, relatively few referrals of parents were made to the parenting group which had no shortage of referrals from other services. The parenting project subsequently expanded its eligibility criteria in order to do more preventative work with parents referred from other agencies. Meanwhile, plans to provide one-to-one work, more fitting to the entrenched problems of young offenders' parents, were shelved. Similarly, the mentoring scheme expanded in new directions and as a result had less room for YOT referrals.

A popular project may be in such demand that the YOT, as just one of the agencies making use of it, may hardly get a look in. For example, the mentoring scheme built up a waiting list, leaving the YOT with a smaller piece of the mentoring cake. In this case, the narrowing down of provision was not for want of YOT referrals. For some other projects, however, the rule of 'use it or lose it' seemed to apply. Contracts were not renewed when the referral numbers did not represent value for money.

When a project is not used it might be because practitioners are failing to take advantage of it or it might be because the projects are not publicising their services well enough. The more sought-after projects had zealous leaders who gave talks to YOT staff and produced newsletters. Publicity, though, is not enough. Clarity of purpose and relevance to the problems of YOT clients are also important factors that influence whether or not referrals are made. For example, perspectives on the purpose of the motor project were foggy because the programme had expanded to include other subjects. Information exchange about the people who are referred to a programme is also another obvious factor in ensuring the best use of projects. This cuts both ways. YOT officers and project staff are equally busy and each side may have wrongly assumed that the other would take the initiative in communicating about a mutual client's progress. The mental health project was an example of good practice in reciprocal communication to inform their respective roles. It may be significant here that the latter was a YOT-dedicated service. Developing YOT-dedicated projects is one sure way of reserving space for YOT clients. Such arrangements provide quicker access to specialist interventions. On the other hand, projects that are exclusively for the YOT and which take on problems normally the province of another service - such as the dyslexia of a child who has not been attending school - may be relieving those services of their own responsibilities for tackling the problem. Practitioners in OYOT suggested that the reforms to youth justice left a hole in social service provision for the welfare needs of children and adolescents. Following the reformation of youth justice, they were required to narrow their focus to offending behaviour. But who was looking after all the other social and family problems, not necessarily related to offending, that previously would have been part of youth justice workers' ambit? It is equally possible that the rearrangements of services that has taken place, with services merging and crossing over may have created gaps. Likewise, a YOT's efforts to supplement the services of another agency may result in that other agency abdicating its own responsibilities. Unfortunately, multi-agency youth offending teams may be perceived, wrongly, as having everything covered.

CHAPTER 8

Linking Custody to Community:
Interventions at the 'Heavy' End

Various statements in both the White Paper *No More Excuses* and the framework document for the Crime and Disorder Act show that the government saw custodial sentences as having a number of functions:

> *Young people who ignore the help offered them, and continue to offend regardless, should be in no doubt about the tough penalties that they will face - including custody if that is necessary to protect the public.*
>
> (Home Office, 1997c: 5.1)

> *The Government believes that a custodial sentence should not be an end in itself - it protects the public by removing the young offender from the opportunity to offend, but the fundamental aim of both custodial and community sentences, in line with the aim of the youth justice system, should be to prevent offending. The Government wants to see constructive regimes, including education and a high standard of care, to help give young offenders a better chance of staying out of trouble once released.*
>
> (Home Office, 1997c: para. 6.5)

> *For those whose offending is serious or persistent, custody may, however, be the only way of protecting the public from further offending. It may be the best way of bringing home to the young person the seriousness of his or her behaviour and the best way of preventing the young person from continuing to offend. Placing a young person in a secure environment that provides discipline, structure, education and training, as well as programmes to tackle offending behaviour, may provide a vital opportunity for the young person to break out of a pattern of offending and regain control of his or her behaviour. Good quality custodial facilities, as well as community based provision, need to be an integral part of youth justice services so that the youth justice system can intervene effectively with all children and young people who offend.*
>
> (Home Office, 1998: para. 9)

Thus custodial sentences for juveniles were envisaged as having multiple purposes: an expression of public disapproval; a deterrent punishment; public protection by incarceration; and rehabilitation via education and 'care'. The relevant sentence introduced to carry the weight of achieving all of these ends was the detention and training order (DTO), half to be served in custody and half to be served in the community.

This chapter looks at the early efforts to implement these new custodial sentences and to join them up with provision in the community, and at problems which got in the way - not least, excessive imposition of the sentence. Measures to reduce the use of custody, to improve standards and to develop a suitable community alternative for serious and persistent offenders are also considered.

Box 8: Detention and training orders

The DTO replaced both the order for Detention in a Young Offender Institution and the Secure Training Order. It came into force as a single, uniform sentence in April 2000 for young offenders aged 15-17 and for 12-14 year-old 'persistent offenders' (a term not defined in the legislation). Under the new legislation, young offenders below the age of 18 cannot be sentenced to imprisonment in adult prisons. From the age of 12 upwards they may receive a DTO for a period of 4-12 months (Powers of Criminal (Sentencing) Act 2000, sections 90 and 91). The first half of a DTO is served in detention - usually in a YOI for those aged 15-17, and in a Secure Training Centre (STC) for those who are under the age of 15. The second half of the sentence is served in the community under the close supervision of a youth offending team. Provision was made within the Powers of Criminal (Sentencing) Act 2000 for the DTO to be extended by order of the Home Secretary to include 10 and 11 year olds. Long term detention for exceptionally serious offences has not been affected by the introduction of DTOs, and remains available to the crown courts under section 53 of the Children and Young Persons Act 1933. 'Young adults' aged 18-20 are now liable to sentences of imprisonment served in adult prisons because, following the recommendation that children under 18 should be dealt with separately from those aged 18 and over (HMIP Thematic Inspection, 1997), the government abolished the sentence of Detention in a Young Offender Institution for this age group.

National standards for DTOs require a 'training plan' for the custodial phase of the sentence to be drawn up within five working days of admission to secure accommodation. Planning meetings should include prison staff, the community YOT officer, the offender and his or her primary carer. The plan, which should regularly be reviewed, should specify objectives to be achieved during the period of detention and training, and how they will be measured.

The 'seamless' sentence

The principal sentence to be utilised in the transformation of custodial provision for young people was the new detention and training order (see Box 8). In theory, at least, this was a prototype for the 'seamless custodial sentence' now introduced for adult offenders (Home Office, 2002b; Home Office, 2003) in which elements served in prison are joined-up with elements served in the community. The sentence planning covers both halves of the sentence and there should be continuity between the activities and provisions of the custodial and the community elements. The DTO made it necessary for prison to look outwards to the community and secure connections between the YOI and the community. In turn it required YOT staff, who are responsible for supervision during the second half of the sentence, to interweave the achievements of the custodial half with the subsequent programme. The challenge for YOTs therefore was to find the best means of becoming involved in all aspects.

For OYOT the necessary co-ordination was realised in the form of staff secondments to the local YOI (Huntercombe). A partnership was formed whereby three members of YOT staff were based for most or half of their time in the YOI, which paid for their salaries. The governor at that time saw the introduction of the DTOs and the setting up of YOTs as the start of a new era in which they would be focussing mainly on taking juveniles (under the age of 18) subject to DTOs and in which it would be fundamental to link sentence planning to services in the community:

> We hope to model what I would simplify as being the continuity in people working with the kids - the paperwork around the kids and the programmes that the kids participate in, all seems to be important if we are to take our place in the new secure system...It is all very well for us to have something done in here - we assess them, we get them onto the various rungs of the ladder in terms of getting used to education - and then the day that they are discharged comes, and have we actually managed to get them reintegrated?...We've got the right sort of structure now and that's what we should be doing. There should be people in here who can see them out there and who know them and carry on when they're discharged. The paperwork and the programmes all ought to be sort of dovetailed, so if they've done up to session five of a ten session course when they leave here, they ought to be able to do session six when they get out in the community.
>
> (YOI governor)

The seconded staff were referred to as the 'DTO team' (though they also worked with section 53 detainees - see Box 8) and, in effect, became an additional unit or arm of the YOT. A casework team, which had previously been developed in the YOI, was facing a greatly expanded workload to meet the needs of a younger prison population. The YOT secondees therefore began with two main tasks:

> It's a combination really. I want them to come in here and to, as it were, model and provide supervision for my casework team so that the approach we take in individual casework will be developed in here. And then also they would provide the through-care for all lads from [the area covered by their YOT]. And if there is a lad here from [the area covered by their YOT] one of the YOT workers will oversee their supervision for the second part of the sentence...Ultimately, if you've managed the community-prison concept, then it ought to work.
>
> (YOI governor)

In accordance with this 'seamless sentence' model, the possibility was also mooted that prison staff, too, could become involved in supervising young people during the post-release half of the sentence. This did not materialise, partly because of other demands on their time but also, it was suggested, because the transition from working with a 'captive' client group to community work with relatively 'free' agents was too great. The model encompassed the three main stages (for more detail see Fransham, 2002):

- *Pre-sentence*: The DTO team liaised closely with the bail support team; they received advance warning of potential custodial sentences in order to conduct joint vulnerability assessments for remand and custody cases; and they helped prepare young people and their families for the possibility of a custodial sentence.
- *Custody*: Once a young person from their local area arrived in custody, they were interviewed on reception by a seconded YOT member from the DTO team. The seconded YOT member then continued as the caseworker and sentence-manager, liaising with family members and external agencies and linking the young person into post-release interventions in the community.
- *Post-custody*: Following custody, the main aims of the DTO team were to support young people and their families as they returned to the community, attend community reviews with external YOT staff, and act as supervising officers for the community element of the sentence.

The rationale for the creation of a casework team, in addition to the usual provision of prison staff 'personal officers' based on the wings, was they would be able to adopt a more child focused approach, free from the pressures and distractions of events on the wings. The manager of the casework team explained that expecting 'personal officers' to be solely responsible for a young person's sentence plan and reviews had been unrealistic in the case of a juvenile population 'because there are so many other things that are involved, like home relationships, education, and there may be protection issues and local authority care issues'. Accordingly, the team was remodelled as a multi-professional team including probation officers, psychologists, education and Connexions staff, the YOT secondees as well as prison officers. A caseworker's responsibilities included: agreeing a DTO 'training plan' with the young person; managing and co-ordinating the plan; writing reports and case records; liaising with outside agencies; and holding monthly reviews and pre-discharge reviews in accordance with national standards. Parents or carers were invited to attend review meetings and caseworkers also carried out one-to-one work with young people and liaised with family members during the custodial element of the sentence (Fransham, 2002). Although imprisonment was generally deplored as a 'destructive awful experience that should be the end of the line', on the positive side it was identified as a period which was conducive to rehabilitative work because, as one of the caseworkers explained:

> For quite a lot of young people, it is a very natural period of reflection. It is a context, which you can, if you have a relationship with them, engage in a more therapeutic social work relationship than you have out here. Because you are not prosecuting them, you are not wearing a justice-type hat, you can do quite a lot of the welfare-hat bit.

The seconded YOT staff were drawn much more widely into the work of the institution beyond their contribution on the casework team. For example, they were frequently consulted on legal matters and on health and social welfare issues affecting children, or asked to step in to talk to detainees in segregation who were refusing to communicate with prison staff. They contributed to developmental work within the prison and were recognised by other staff as having broken down some barriers between prison officers and other prison staff, and introduced a child centred perspective. In particular, they helped to establish co-ordinated child protection policies, for example clarifying procedures for the monitoring of phone calls and drawing up protocols for the early identification of young people who have been the victims of abuse or who are especially vulnerable.

How well did this grand design work out in practice? In interviews with trainees, prison staff, caseworkers and YOT staff, the overriding impression was that great strides had been taken to provide constructive sentences and the benefits were being reaped. Nearly all of the trainees who we interviewed were receiving education or training and spoke of their sentence targets and post-release plans, and most of them identified ways in which they had been helped by their caseworker. Former youth justice staff compared the new community-integrated arrangements very favourably with previous custodial provision:

Three years ago you would never have got to see them inside apart from half an hour and there would be little time to do any of the planning work.

The needs of young people are now far more tailored than they would have been. A major positive I think is having the forum where the parents and YOT worker who have most knowledge about a young person are present. In most cases it is the YOT worker that is chairing the meeting and contributing most.

The seconded YOT staff drew attention to some of the administrative difficulties in operating DTOs. For example, target setting was often problematic because staff had not been trained in the selection of appropriate targets: they would use broad concepts like 'increase victim awareness' without specifying how that could be measured. Assessment information from field staff was often not available at the time when young people were admitted. Set against these frustrations and their perceptions of excessive and inappropriate imposition of custodial sentences, the seconded YOT staff pointed to advantages of DTOs over previous custodial sentences for young people:

It is still early days, but if I had to jump one side of the fence I would say it is definitely a better deal for young people. The paper work is awkward but it does insist on people thinking more creatively about that sentence and tying people into doing things and everybody is co-opted into the sentence planning in a way that didn't happen before.

The kids like seeing the YOT workers monthly - definitely like having that number of visits. Parents feel more involved.

Monthly reviews, although they are a nightmare to organise and they are a very heavy workload, they are brilliant. The kids get a clear understanding of their progress or lack of progress and where that is, and they can then pull it up. And I've seen kids, who have struggled in custody, start to excel because they feel somehow they can own it. It has given them some ownership in terms of trying to do things that I don't think was there before. The month early release is a fantastic carrot.

The early period of planning and implementing the DTOs therefore was encouraging, with practice in some YOIs contrasting favourably with conditions prior to the reforms. In 1997, a thematic review on *Young Prisoners* by Her Majesty's Inspectorate of Prisons had condemned custodial institutions for young offenders as 'warehousing' them rather than educating and training them and meeting their needs. Following the implementation of reforms and the introduction of DTOs, the Chief Inspector continued to be generally censorious of the regimes he inspected but he was encouraged by some of the developments. He criticised the YJB for being more concerned with how much was done (quantities and time factors) rather than with 'how' (the quality of processes and outcomes). However, he praised YJB policies for 'opening up' the prison service to closer working relationships with additional agencies and he was encouraged by the inter-agency work between YOI staff and YOT workers, the development of casework and the involvement of families in case reviews. He concluded that:

While there is a long way to go, I find it most encouraging that so much has been achieved in less than a year. Those who question whether this is so should consider that they would not even have been able to think of the question a year ago, and what they are doing is not so much questioning provision but details about something that is now being provided'

(Ramsbotham, 2001: 21)

A study commissioned by the YJB to evaluate progress in delivering DTOs identified the following elements of best practice within the YOIs investigated: an overall pro-social ethos; good educational and work activities; promotion of healthy peer group interactions; provision of opportunities to develop self esteem and re-sponsibility; assistance with resisting drugs; and creating links with families (Hazel et al., 2002).

Coming apart at the seams

Despite the promising beginnings described above, the overall situation in YOIs was far from satisfactory. Progress in implementing the 'seamless sentence' was greatly impeded by a number of interrelated factors: 'demand' for training resources exceeding 'supply'; staff shortages and regime problems; and an alarming influx of inmates.

Stretched resources and failing standards

A major practical problem against implementing DTOs as intended was that there were not enough staff and resources to meet the 'demand'. A high turnover of staff plus the rising trainee population meant that resources were overstretched and exasperated staff had insufficient time to liaise with caseworkers and to work with the young people: 'The YJB have got this idealistic dream which we support but we haven't got the resources to do it'. A clash of cultures between prison and non-prison staff also hindered progress. For YOT staff, the 'security first' culture of the prison detracted from the other goals to be achieved.

Not least among the barriers against implementing a constructive custodial sentence were the conditions and standards of administration and care in young offender institutions. A thematic review by the prison service inspectorate reported lamentably poor conditions, regimes and training programmes running throughout the custodial provision for young offenders (HMIP, 1997). The White Paper *No More Excuses* had referred to custodial arrangements for 10-17 year olds at that time as 'chaotic and dysfunctional' (Home Office, 1997c: para. 6.2) and it noted great variability in the quality and costs of regimes and in the availability of secure accommodation for young offenders. By 1998, the government had concluded that there existed 'no definable juvenile secure estate' and that 'fundamental change' was necessary if children's needs and offending behaviour were to be addressed (Home Office, 1998). This was the situation into which detention and training orders were introduced.

The YOI with which OYOT had gone into partnership was at the time a 'cut above' most of the rest. It had enjoyed a period of stability under a visionary head governor and it had been highly praised following inspections. However, the switch to a primarily younger population, subject to new legislation, and with the intake numbers ever swelling, took its toll. As the number of custodial sentences rose, staffing problems increased and standards fell. Communication within the institution and between staff and outside personnel deteriorated because of the workload being carried on all sides. A subsequent inspection report identified groundbreaking child protection procedures, excellent links between caseworkers and YOTs with good sentence planning. Nevertheless, it described the YOI as a 'fragmented establishment' in which there was insufficient liaison and co-operation between departments and groups, inadequate education provision which met the needs of only half of the population and insufficient constructive activity available to young people (HMIP, 2001). An examination of the inspection reports for other YOIs around this time suggests that delivery of DTOs rarely lived up to the ideal.

A bulging trainee population

The main stumbling blocks were the rising inmate population and increased admission of young people for whom custody seemed especially inappropriate. Statistics showed increases were much steeper in some areas than in others, raising the spectre of 'sentencing by geography'. While the recorded rates of youth offending for under-18s fell by a fifth between 1992 and 2001, the numbers going into custody steadily increased. Between March and June 2000 the sentenced population in the juvenile secure estate increased by 14 per cent (Bateman, 2001). Moreover, the influx consisted of increasingly younger 'early stage' offenders - particularly worrying given that the number of under-15s in custody had already increased by 800 per cent over the previous decade (NACRO, 2003). It was also noted that more post-release trainees were being returned to custody for offences committed while on licence. This trend turned a potentially constructive sentence if reserved for 'heavy end' cases (the most serious offences and the most persistent offenders) into one that was counter-productive.

YOT staff were shocked by the sharp rise in the use of custody and by the numbers given detention and training orders for whom it seemed unwarranted. Although, as discussed in Chapter 6, magistrates in the area were adamant that custodial sentences were only imposed when absolutely necessary, there was a shared perception among YOT practitioners, as is evident in the quote below, that magistrates had either become more punitive or less restrained about using custodial sentences than they had been in the pre-DTO era:

> *Certainly kids are getting whacked straight up the tariff for three offences of, for example, shoplifting and an assault and it's eight months in a secure training centre. My concern is if the sentencing criteria are standard and uniform, why are people at a relatively early period in their offending and in their lives being put on DTOs whereas we've got significant offenders with massive offending records only being given four months and they are 17?*

> *It is hard to believe sometimes. You think, are they really, really considering giving someone a DTO for stealing four CDs out of HMV? Perhaps they are! And that's a worrying thing. There does seem to be an inconsistency in the sentencing of younger and older offenders and a tendency to give DTOs prematurely. There's almost an eagerness to dish out DTOs.*

As a result staff in the YOI noticed significant changes in the inmate population, as explained most graphically in the following interview extracts:

> *The biggest changes are the increase in first-time, out-of-nowhere young people, in that previously kids would have gone through a whole series of court proceedings. That doesn't happen anymore. They come very quickly into custody - and it is a shock. We get a lot of kids very distressed, shocked, families shocked, saying 'I can't believe this has happened!', very un-streetwise young people - a high increase in vulnerable young people.*

> *The other big change we have seen is the amount of aggrieved young people coming in with their lack of remand time. They don't feel the courts take remand time into consideration properly. They don't get bail for a day anymore and they come in through the door very pissed off. Things start with nothing to ameliorate them, and for short orders there is no hope of doing any work with them. So you have a very disgruntled, unhappy, already difficult, young person for a short period of time. The assault rates and incident rates have escalated.*

I am very concerned about the number of youngsters coming back on recall for relatively minor offences when they've done fairly well on the actual licence - so it's the offence that has triggered the recall and not their response to the licence. Obviously it is within the powers of the courts to do but - it's like the action plan order where you are going to do most of your effective work at the early stage - if you pull them back on recall basically they are going to do the whole thing again. It is not tailored to the people who come back because they just go back into the process and start a very short induction and probably end up doing the same courses. I think the message is getting across that the DTO is far more punitive and it lacks the flexibility for discretion at the other end: fail once and that's it, you are recalled.

The knock-on effects of this situation were that instead of the constructive work that had been intended the caseworkers were dealing with an escalating rate of assaults against other trainees and against staff and an increase in self-harming behaviour and suicide attempts. The nature of the work became comparable to that in a remand centre because of the constant changes in the population, with young people coming in from and going out to courts every day. The YOI was filled to capacity and plans to prioritise local lads in the intake had to be abandoned because of the increased need for YOI beds from other areas.

Why had there been such a dramatic rise? The increased powers to impose custody given to magistrates, and the climate of popular punitiveness are commonly put forward as contributory factors. Staff who attributed the popularity of the DTO to its having been 'sold by the YJB as a positive piece of sentencing' and the 'belief among magistrates that you go into custody and you come out educated' perhaps came closest to putting their finger on it. In many cases though, educational provision was proving to be very limited. As one practitioner stated: 'They get the detention alright but the training doesn't happen'. This applied particularly to those on short sentences or returned following a breach because 'things don't kick-in in time', and even if sentence planning had taken place and some relevant contacts with outside services had been made, there had not been enough opportunity to engage the young person's interest nor to carry plans forward.

Reducing the use of custody

England and Wales, since the early 1990s, has had a much higher proportion of young people in prison service custody than other European countries (Bateman, 2001). Yet the United Nations Convention on the Rights of the Child requires that custody for under 18 year-olds should be used as a last resort and for the shortest possible time. Sir David Ramsbotham, who was the Chief Inspector of Prisons during the formative period for the new youth justice, consistently expressed the view that 'children should not be held in Prison Service custody [although] that is not to say that some children should not be in custody, but that it should be differently provided' (Ramsbotham, 2001: 21).

The Chief Inspector's view that prison is no place for children and that custody should be reserved for the 'acute' part of a broader system focussed on rehabilitation was widely shared by staff we interviewed within the YOI. Indeed, it was those who were the most involved in reforming the provision for young people in YOIs and most enthusiastic about the potential of DTOs who were most vehement about the harms that imprisonment could bring:

> *I feel passionately about the deal that young people get in prison. I think they are treated abominably. They are dumped and then forgotten by the outside agencies. It gives them breathing space, and nobody does anything constructive. It is a very harmful experience for young people, especially long-term. And it is only recently that some YOIs have moved to ensure that there is appropriate education and something akin to a timetable so that you have terms and break weeks in terms. But still, the re-integration just doesn't happen, it seems to me. It can be really difficult for them after they come out...it takes six weeks for a kid to get some equilibrium again, by which time the expectations upon them have been excessive and unrealistic...They have failed and they are back in the system. So I feel very strongly that if we are going to do something, we need to try and do something proactively by getting casework sorted whilst they are inside, so that agencies don't forget them.*

The potential impact of a prison sentence at different stages was also brought home to those working within custodial settings. Seconded YOT staff emphasised the prospect of custody would have less of a deterrent impact against future offending once a young person had experienced it:

> *It is society's greatest sanction. If we use it on somebody at 12, what else is there left? Fear is a great motivator. I think fear of custody has always been a fairly good motivator to try and keep kids in the community. If that goes then what? I think it is a bit of a dangerous social experiment to make custody a big positive thing.*

Paradoxically, this may be especially true of those regimes which are the most progressive and advanced in providing constructive activities and ensuring links with families and outside services.

The response of the YJB to rising custodial figures plus wide differences in the custodial sentencing trends in different parts of the country - what has been termed 'justice by geography' - was to introduce league tables which 'named and shamed' the worst areas. Youth courts were called upon to cut down the number of short custodial sentences and to make more use of new community penalties. The YJB's policy statement (which can be seen on its website) includes a commitment to reducing the use of custody. Significantly, when the YJB brought out performance measures, one of them was to reduce the number of custodial remands and sentences (see Box 10, Measure 4) and the targets set for December 2004 are to:

- Reduce the number of remands to the secure estate as a proportion of all remands (excluding bail) to 30 per cent.
- Reduce the number of custodial sentences as a proportion of all court disposals to 6 per cent.

Although on face value this appears to be imposing on YOTs a requirement over which they have no control, they can influence custody rates in various ways; for example, by making sure that alternatives to custody are suggested in their court reports and having a policy, when writing pre-sentence reports, of never proposing custodial sentences (Bateman, 2001). The challenge to youth offending teams is to do their part in providing high standard, well resourced services to support community alternatives.

Improving the standard

By 1998, the government had concluded that there existed 'no definable juvenile secure estate' and that 'fundamental change' was necessary to co-ordinate the identification of placements and to introduce and monitor standards (Home Office, 1998). Subsequently, the Youth Justice Board was made the central co-ordinating body for the entire juvenile secure estate, including young offender institutions, secure training centres and local authority secure children's homes. Provision of custodial placements remained under the remit of the owners of the three separate systems (the Prison Service, Home Office and Department of Health respectively), but the YJB established a purchasing and commissioning role for placements ('beds') in which to put young people subject to a custodial sentence. In addition, the Board took on the responsibility for setting regime standards for the juvenile secure estate.

Developing a better alternative

In addition to the steps taken, as mentioned above, to bring down the proportions of custodial sentences and to improve provision within the secure estate, the YJB has increasingly promoted the Intensive Supervision and Surveillance Programme - an intervention introduced after the Crime and Disorder Act 1998 - aimed at persistent young offenders and those who have committed the most serious offences (see Box 9).

Box 9: Intensive supervision and surveillance programmes

Community-based 'Intensive Supervision and Surveillance Programmes' (ISSPs) were launched by the Youth Justice Board in selected areas across England and Wales in July 2001. With an eye to the three per cent of persistent offenders who commit approximately a quarter of all offences (Graham and Bowling, 1995), a £45 million three-year programme 'to tackle hardcore repeat young offenders' was implemented by the Board in 41 areas (YJB News, October 2000: 1). To date, in England and Wales, it is the most rigorous non-custodial intervention that has been made available for young people. It targets the most prolific and serious young offenders, who have been charged, warned or convicted at least four times within a 12-month period, and who have received at least one previous community or custodial penalty. ISSPs effectively consist of a mix of intensive monitoring of the young offender's movements and whereabouts by means such as electronic tagging and telephone monitoring

---

using voice verification technology, as well as an intensive supervisory syllabus of education and training, restorative justice and offending behaviour work (Home Office, 2001). All these services are co-ordinated by the local youth offending team.

The Youth Justice Board set three key objectives for ISSPs:

- To reduce the rate of reoffending in the target group of offenders by five per cent and reduce the seriousness of any reoffending.
- To tackle underlying problems of the young people concerned in an effective manner with a particular emphasis on educational needs.
- To demonstrate that supervision and surveillance is being undertaken consistently and rigorously, and in ways which will reassure the community and sentencers of their credibility and likely success.

Interim findings from the national evaluation of the ISSP revealed that out of 1,464 ISSPs imposed up to September 2002, 64 per cent were part of a supervision order, 16 per cent were attached to a DTO, 15 per cent to bail and six per cent to a community rehabilitation order (11 per cent were subject to more than one order). Notably, 61 per cent of the young offenders were tagged, while voice verification was used in 24 per cent of cases, and 61 per cent of the offenders were also 'tracked' by ISSP staff. In an interim report to the YJB, the evaluators reported that the initial analysis of reconviction at the six-month point for a small sample suggested that ISSPs could be having an impact on the frequency of recorded offending. The mean number of recorded offences fell from 5.4 to 2.5. The evaluators stressed though that it was too early to draw any firm conclusions on the impact of ISSP on reconviction (Waters et al., 2003).

Reduction in the use of custodial sentencing was not initially specified as one of the objectives of the ISSP. Soon after its introduction, however, and in response to soaring numbers of short-term DTOs for low and medium risk offenders, the ISSP was publicised by the YJB and by ministers as 'a robust alternative to custodial sentences'. It was as a positive alternative to custody that the ISSP was received by YOT practitioners, although at first they were daunted by the introduction of yet another initiative and thought that some of their most intensive and effective work was about to be taken over by a specialist team. Once the ISSPs had been running for some time, practitioners who had objected to electronic monitoring in principle, came round to defending it as being less of an infringement on liberty than custody and providing a structure to a young person's routine (Moore, 2004). In our own discussions with YOT staff examples were given of how the 'tag' had made it easier for young people to resist peer pressure to go out and commit further crime.

Following the introduction of ISSPs the local statistics on the proportions of court appearances resulting in custody showed a reduction to 6.9 per cent, bettering the YJB's target of 6 per cent. Recently, the former Chairman of the Youth Justice Board announced that the ISSP should replace the short DTO as a sentence of the court which can be imposed for up to a maximum of 12 months: 'This would be much more effective than short custodial sentences which disrupt lives and offer limited opportunities to address the causes of offending behaviour' (Warner, 2003). There are dangers though that these aspirations may not be met. While ISSPs may in the short term have the effect of bringing down custodial rates, if they are recommended and imposed indiscriminately and if breach procedures are applied inflexibly, they could result in greater use of custody over the long term (Cavadino and Dignan, 2002: 304).

CHAPTER 9

What has Been Achieved?
Outcomes and Implementation

Three years after the youth offending teams came into being, and following favourable Home Office figures on reconviction rates, the chief executive of the YJB announced that there had been 'more progress in preventing re-offending by children and young people in the youth justice system than anyone expected' (Perfect, 2003). The Prime Minister Tony Blair sent his congratulations to the YJB, declaring that the fall in reconviction rates for young offenders showed 'how much can be achieved if we remove the obstacles and barriers to us all working together. It's a lesson we must put into practice right across the criminal justice system' (Blair, 2003: 6). The message to the public, therefore, was that the multi-agency approach plus the implementation of the Crime and Disorder Act and subsequent legislation had been a success in youth justice.

In this chapter we reflect on the extent to which our findings from this in-depth study of a youth offending system support this official declaration of achievement. First we consider 'success' in terms of reconviction rates which were announced two years after the new youth justice had been set in place. Then we look at the achievement of the objectives and targets set for youth justice, drawing especially on the experiences in the pathfinder YOT which was the subject of this study. We conclude the chapter by raising a broader question: What kind of a youth justice system do we now have at the start of the 21st century?

Reoffending and reconviction rates

Prima facie, the most obvious and direct way to gauge whether the new measures have achieved their main aim of reducing recidivism is to refer to comparative reconviction data. Is the reconviction rate for children and young people who have been recipients of specific interventions lower than the reconviction rate for young people with the same profile who have not received such interventions? We all know that lower reconviction following an intervention could be attributable to many other variables instead of, or as well as, the intervention. Furthermore, reconviction rates are just a proxy for a higher, but unknown, level of reoffending. Nevertheless, decreases and increases in reconviction rates provide one source of potentially useful information about change in offending behaviour, even though the underlying causes of such change remain unclear (Kershaw, 1999).

The analysis of juvenile reconviction rates by the Home Office Research, Development and Statistics Directorate showed a reduction of 14.6 per cent in relative terms compared against the reconviction rates for 1997 (Jennings, 2003). The difference between the rates for 1997 and 2000 worked out as a 22.5 per cent proportionate reduction in reconviction rates - well in excess of the target of a five per cent reduction set out in the Public Service Agreement. The greatest reduction was for first-time offenders: reconviction rates fell from 21.2 per cent to 12.4 per cent - a proportionate reduction of 41 per cent, suggesting that the policy of 'nipping crime in the bud' really had worked.

The claims made on the basis of these findings have been criticised as unreliable because the 1997 sample had different criminal histories. Also factors such as the speeding up of justice and the significant changes to the criteria for police and court disposals render such comparisons less convincing. Some Home Office researchers have previously argued against the use of reconviction as a proxy for a comparison group (Kershaw, 1999). The YJB has tended to spin small signs of promise into large placards of success. When the national evaluators of restorative justice projects noted in a *draft* report that a sample of young people who had received restorative justice interventions had a slightly lower reconviction rate than the Home Office sample, they added a caveat to point out that the Home Office sample was not an adequate comparison group and this meant that the results *could not* be taken as an indication that restorative justice had been effective (Wilcox, 2003). Nevertheless this finding was referred to in the YJB's Annual Review as showing that 'using restorative methods in treating early offenders does decrease both the likelihood of further offending and its seriousness' (YJB, 2002: 13). A similarly selective use was made of the reports of other national evaluations of YJB development projects.

Even in cases where it has been possible to carry out rigorous evaluations making use of suitable comparison groups, reconviction studies as a measure of 'what works' in reducing offending have serious limitations. Most obviously, not all offences are detected, and not all charges lead to convictions. In 2000-2001 out of 12.9 million recorded crimes 1.02 million (7.9 per cent) were 'brought to justice' - in other words, they led to a caution, conviction or were 'taken into consideration' as part of a sentence (Home Office, 2002). Reconviction data are therefore a proxy for reoffending data which is much more difficult to obtain.

Asking young people to self-report their offending is another source of information about reoffending - one which is potentially unreliable but which is likely to be a more accurate reflection of reoffending than reconviction rates for reasons already given. Surveys of offending by young people based on self-report consistently reveal that high percentages of them have committed offences that have not been detected, in addition to any that have led to convictions (Graham and Bowling, 1995; Flood-Page et al., 2000). Studies that have compared self-reported convictions and officially recorded offending for the same group have, however, shown that they tend to increase or decrease in the same direction and so it is generally agreed that the two approaches are complementary (Tarling, 1993). It is therefore reasonable to utilise one of these approaches in the absence of the other as an indicator of the direction of change in offending behaviour.

The overall reconviction rates in the pathway YOT were in keeping with the national trend. In 2001, data monitored by the YOT showed a 3.5 per cent reduction in the number of offences committed by young people in the county. Individual reconviction data were not available to us when we carried out this study but we drew on self-report and qualitative information for some early indications of the impact of interventions on reoffending rates.

Self-report data were obtained from 60 young people, who were first interviewed at the start of a disposal or order and then re-interviewed several months later either during the period of intervention or after being dealt with by the YOT. In the later interviews they were asked whether they had reoffended since the first interview and, if so, whether the offences had led to convictions. Two thirds of the sample said they had committed one or more further offences. However, considerably fewer (22 per cent of the sample and a third of those who had reoffended) had received further convictions. That is, as might be expected, the majority of offences had either not been detected or had not yet led to court proceedings.

In interviews at the start of a court order, or at the time of the final warning, 17 per cent (N = 60) said there was zero chance of them committing another offence in the next 12 months, but 40 per cent said there was more than a medium chance they would commit an offence in the next 12 months. Eighty-five per cent admitted, in response to questioning, that one or more factors could make it difficult for them to desist from further offending. The most frequently mentioned obstacles against desistance and the percentage who identified them as factors that would make if difficult for them to 'stay away from crime' were as follows:

Encouragement or pressure from mates	60%
Knowing it is easy money	58%
Boredom or need for excitement	50%
Retaliation or self-defence when provoked or attacked	52%

Usually a combination of such risk factors was mentioned as relevant to the risk of reoffending, but when asked to identify which was the '*main* thing making it hard to avoid crime' the most frequently selected risk factor was 'encouragement from mates': 30 per cent picked this out as the *main* factor. Likewise, the most mentioned 'protective' factor, when they were asked about how they could best avoid further offending, was to keep away from certain mates and co-offenders. In second and third interviews with some of the sample, a high proportion of them reported further offending that had not at that time been detected or led to court proceedings.

This was a very small sample and therefore the findings are easy to dismiss - though it is unlikely that these discrepancies between self-reported reoffending and reconviction data were any different to figures that might have been obtained elsewhere, given the usual gap between self-reported reoffending and reconviction records. Such self-report interview data are sobering when set against the jubilant headlines of the *Youth Justice News*. However, they need not call into question the overall positive implications of official reconviction data, nor the local reconviction data which corresponded with the national trend. Reoffending behaviour and reconviction rates in the short-term may belie progress that has been made towards desistance or towards reduced criminality. The frequency and the nature of further offending should also be taken into account, as well as changes in a range of factors associated with crime, such as attitudes towards crime and lifestyle patterns. Indeed, such *relative* changes were identified by YOT workers when asked to identify 'successes' in their caseloads for the evaluation. Rather than choosing absolute desisters, they pulled out case files for young people who had reoffended following the YOT's intervention to illustrate effective work. For the more seriously troubled young people with whom they work, they had relatively low - but arguably realistic - expectations, and therefore felt rewarded by moderate improvements. The following comment was typical of the philosophical perspective taken by staff engaged in supervising young people:

> *Don't let us lose sight that sometimes these kids are in such a state that nothing is going to work for a while, so you have to make your 'what works' agenda small and piecemeal to get a kid from one step to another.*

(YOT worker)

It is perfectly reasonable that practitioners helping very troubled and damaged young people to cope with the 'complexity and vicissitudes of real life' (Eadie and Canton, 2002) regard practical achievements, such as improved accommodation and reconciliation with a parent, as significant progress - even if another court appearance may be pending. It is clear from research on criminal careers (Farrington, 1996) and research on desistance (Maruna, 2000) that persistent young offenders who began offending early ('early onset') will not suddenly stop overnight and that a whole person approach, addressing 'needs as well as deeds', is appropriate to bring 'change out of chaos' (McNeill and Bachelor, 2002). Reconviction rates over the short term will be a poor reflection of considerable work being undertaken to make progress through the vital preliminary stages of the change process.

Achieving the objectives of the youth justice system

The Youth Justice Board applies 13 performance measures to make annual assessments of the achievement of YOTs (See Box 10). Specified targets each year are linked to each measure. For example, measure 8, as described in the YJB guidance to YOTs for updating for their youth justice plans, specifies that, by 2004:

- *All young people who are assessed by Asset as manifesting acute mental health difficulties should be referred by YOTs to the Child and Mental Health Services (CAMHS) for a formal assessment commencing within five working days of the receipt of the referral with a view to their accessing a tier three service or other appropriate CAMHS tier service.*
- *All young people who are assessed as having non-acute mental health concerns should be referred by the YOT for an assessment, and engagement by the appropriate CAMHS tier (1-3) should commence in 15 working days.*

Box 10: Performance measures set by the YJB

Measure 1: Reduce the number of young offenders committing offences of domestic burglary, vehicle crime and robbery.

Measure 2: Reduce re-offending rates for pre-court disposals, first tier penalties, community penalties and custodial penalties.

Measure 3: Increase the proportion of final warnings supported by interventions.

Measure 4: Reduce the use of the secure estate for remands and custodial sentences.

Measure 5: Increase the use of restorative justice processes.

Measure 6: Increase the proportion of victims, who have been either consulted or who have participated in restorative processes, who are either satisfied or very satisfied with the outcome.

Measure 7: Increase parental satisfaction (statutory and voluntary parenting programmes).

Measure 8: Ensure Asset is completed for all young people subject to community disposals end custodial sentences.

Measure 9: Ensure 90 per cent of pre-sentence reports are submitted within the prescribed timescales.

Measure 10: Ensure that all initial training plans for young people subject to Detention and Training Orders are drawn up within timescales prescribed by National Standards.

Measure 11: Increase the percentage of young people supervised by the YOT who are either in full-time education, training or employment:

Measure 12: Ensure that all young people either subject to final warnings with an intervention, community interventions or custodial sentences, have on completion satisfactory accommodation to go to.

Measure 13: Ensure that young people who are assessed by Asset as manifesting mental health difficulties receive speedy formal assessment by appropriate mental health specialists.

The extent to which specific YOTs have been able to reach these targets each year can be scrutinised by access to their annual youth justice plan, many of which are now available on-line. A more illuminating way for us to review the early achievements and the problems encountered is to return to the objectives that were set for youth offending teams by the YJB. These objectives - originally termed 'principles', which is probably a better description - were listed in Box 2. We have already looked in previous chapters at some of the work undertaken to address each of these, but here draw together perspectives on the extent to which they have been accomplished and the issues they have raised.

Speeding up the administration of justice

The government made a pledge in 1997 that, in the case of persistent young offenders, it would halve the average time from arrest to sentence from an average of 142 days to an average of 71 days. This was achieved ahead of the target date, and by the end of the financial year 2002/03 the average time was down to 69 days (YJB, 2003). For OYOT, after 18 months in operation, the average number of days had gone down from 140 days to 87 days. This was encouraging progress though still some way off the target.

In practical terms, reaching this point has required better co-ordination between agencies and the streamlining of systems, including fast tracking of persistent young offenders. It has also required a culture change within the court system, from an unquestioning acceptance of delays to monitored procedures influenced by schedules and performance management. Few would argue with the underlying objective to reach decisions speedily enough for them to be perceived by the young person as a direct response to their offending behaviour. Magistrates and youth justice practitioners, on the whole, supported this principle and, therefore accepted the extra pressure placed upon them in order to meet it. However, some possible costs were anticipated, and these became manifest once the faster system got into motion.

The main gain, and the point of speeding things up, is that criminal justice disposals are meted out for each offence much sooner: committing an offence has clearly related consequences and the young person and others will not therefore conclude that they have 'got away with it'. There have been costs though as well as gains. For a young person who is in a spate of persistent offending, they will go to court more frequently - there could be a separate court appearance for each offence, resulting in acceleration through the sentencing tariff. Under the old system, delays would often mean that several offences, including additional offences following the original charge, would be dealt with collectively when the young person finally got to court. The new system may be unnecessarily interventionist for those young people 'behaving badly' for a brief period during the normal course of growing up. Indeed, there is a danger that too much intervention will be counter-productive because regular court appearances and sentences reinforce a criminal identity and bring the young person into contact with other more serious offenders, whereas most young people mature out of this phase more quickly if criminal justice intervention is kept to a minimum (Goldson, 2000; Muncie, 2001).

Another cost of 'speeding up' identified by YOT workers was that it left insufficient time to seek out additional information which sentencers should have at their disposal. Staff were largely successful in meeting time limits set for the preparation of pre-sentence reports. However, they had the greatest difficulty in finishing assessments and reports for persistent young offenders on whom there is generally more information to process though, paradoxically, less time in which to write reports.

A further 'trade off' against the gains of 'speeding up' applies in particular to final warnings and referral order panels. Requirements to keep within time limits are at cross purposes with the requirement to give victims the opportunity to have their perspective taken into account. The staff admitted that they struggled to get through the necessary work involved in making contact with victims and in getting together relevant victim information in time for meetings.

Punishment proportionate to the crime

The acceleration effect, previously mentioned, is caused by decreased flexibility in decision making at various stages, as well as by the speeding up of criminal proceedings. The combined effect is that more young people go to court after fewer offences, and more offences result in formal proceedings and an intervention. Also, younger children have been appearing in court and more court appearances have led to remands in custody or custodial sentences. The metaphors of 'widening the net' and 'thinning the mesh' were unforgettably used by Stanley Cohen (1985) to describe these processes.

The principle of proportionality - that is, the principle that the punishment should be directly proportional to the seriousness of the crime (von Hirsh, 2001) - is placed at risk by these interventionist trends. Thus, for example, a young person is now likely to receive a programme of rehabilitation as part of a final warning for a minor offence that would previously have resulted in a caution. While the YOT staff may decide that the offence and the young person's circumstances do not necessitate any intervention, performance measure 3 (see Box 10) obliges them to provide it in order to meet their targets.

The need for young people to admit responsibility for offences in order to receive a final warning and a referral order may also result in a disproportionate response. Should a young person deny responsibility for a first offence they will then be catapulted into court even though, perhaps, they have not previously received a final warning or even a reprimand. This is not reversible in the event of later admissions of guilt. Another source of acceleration arises from the removal of the option of the conditional discharge for first court appearances. Magistrates and YOT staff had previously seen this as an appropriate sentence for many first court appearances. The option of an absolute discharge remained available but, in contrast to the conditional discharge, was only appropriate in exceptional cases.

Even if a young person has first gone through the usual pre-court stages of 'reprimand' followed by 'final warning' before getting a referral order, they appear to be used inequitably when referral orders of the same lengths are imposed for offences of low and high gravity. As discussed in Chapter 5, the subsequent contracts agreed at meetings with a youth offender panel, where the young people are not allowed to have legal representation, again, can seem inequitable and the outcomes excessive.

Quite apart from the sense that the punishment is disproportionate when a referral order is given for a minor offence, such as theft of a chocolate bar, staff regard the time that is spent on it as disproportionate. Comments made by magistrates, such as the following, indicated that they tended to agree:

Referral orders are mandatory and I would rather they were optional. Sometimes just a small fine would really be better. Or just a conditional discharge, just 'don't do it again' and go away. But to give them three months of input from the YOT team who are already pretty pressed, well sometimes it seems disproportionate and I personally would like to have choice.

YOT staff were alarmed by the increased number of custodial sentences following the introduction of detention and training orders, especially for younger ages, and viewed the DTO as a sentence which was disproportionate to the seriousness of the offence. Specific examples of this included a case where the young person was given a four month DTO and had an adult co-defendant who was sentenced to 30 days imprisonment.

The issue of disproportionality is an issue of justice: more punishment than the offence deserves is unjust. Incidental issues, however, are whether these sentences cause harm and whether they meet other sentencing objectives. A disproportionate sentence that then harms the offender in some way would be additionally unjust, as well as counter-productive to other objectives. Interventions carry the risk of 'labelling' an individual as an offender and may thereby promote rather than reduce criminality. Whether such instances do indeed have a criminalising effect deserves to be thoroughly investigated.

Confronting offenders with the consequences of their behaviour

Although it was clear that this objective was particularly concerned with the consequences for victims of young offenders, it also alluded to 'the consequences of their offending for themselves and their family' and was aimed at helping them to develop a sense of personal responsibility on the basis that 'If young people understand the consequences of their behaviour, and take personal responsibility for it, they are less likely to repeat it' (Home Office, 1998). However, the notion of confronting young people with what they have done is open to different interpretations, and this objective has tended to be associated with the requirement to hold young people responsible for their behaviour *and then to punish them*. Indeed, some interpretations seem to jump to punishment being the consequence, side-stepping the more literal meaning behind the statement. Staff questioned whether young people should be regarded as responsible agents given their immaturity, especially those in younger age groups. They encountered many examples of such immaturity because the ending of repeat cautioning had resulted in an increase of young people under 14 and 15 in their caseloads.

Practitioners questioned the degree to which this objective had required them to do anything essentially different to their previous practice. Encouraging an awareness of victims and of the consequences of their behaviour for others had always been an element of work with young offenders.

One key difference between previous and revised practice though was increased attention to victim views through victim statements for court reports and, more directly, through victims' attendance at final warning conferences and referral order panels. Much publicity has been given to meetings which take place between victims and offenders, giving the impression that they are routine and commonplace. Our research revealed that such meetings occurred fairly infrequently. Even when victims were willing to come forward and share their perspective, some discretion was needed about whether or not it would be appropriate for the victim to attend a final warning or referral order meeting. As pointed out by a front-line member of staff there was always a danger that meetings could end up being counter-productive:

You need a good quality victim to make it work properly because you know, if you get somebody who wants to exact revenge, you don't let it happen. So it is all very well saying we should have victim and offender meetings but there are actually a very small number of circumstances where it is appropriate and safe. And I don't think we can talk about that very much.

Because victim-offender contacts are a good idea in principle but are hard to achieve in practice, there is a need for more creative ways in which to involve victims. While victim impact statements are read out at meetings, inevitably these are less effective at conveying to the young person what the impact of the offence has been than a face to face meeting would be. One senior practitioner suggested to us that it would be a good idea to make use of audio or video involvement for victims who do not want to be present at meetings so that the emotional content of a victim statement could be more personally conveyed.

Encouraging reparation to victims

The objective of 'confronting young offenders with the consequences of their behaviour' is closely associated with the objective of 'encouraging reparation to victims' but the latter is regarded more positively. Whereas the former is perceived as having punitive overtones, 'encouraging reparation to victims' is the closest that the specified duties come to building-in an explicit restorative justice approach. Equally though, this objective has been viewed as problematic by staff because of the potential conflict with welfare considerations.

The principle of focussing on victims was embraced from the start and a carefully co-ordinated reparation programme was developed under the dedicated and creative leadership of the co-ordinator. The reparation scheme resulted in diverse projects for indirect reparation, (for examples see 'Making amends' in Chapter 6). A victim liaison team, headed by a former employee of Victim Support was appointed, and a victim policy was drawn up to specify priorities and principles in relation to victims and to stress the importance attached to victim issues (See Chapter 4). Strenuous efforts were made to involve victims at both the final warning stage and in referral order panels, but the reparation project included few opportunities for direct reparation and if it did take place, it was generally only in the form of an apology, either face to face or by letter.

The issues of (a) who should contact victims and (b) the form that contact should take were problematic. The majority of victims approached did not want to attend meetings with the offender. Different methods of making contact and of encouraging the attendance of victims raised ethical questions about whether the burden of assumption about attendance should be placed onto victims. To add to the complications during the early stages, even though a victim liaison officer had been appointed, the police procedures for data protection prevented her from initiating contact with victims. There was in general a lack of clarity about how the YOT should be working with victims, despite a pronounced managerial commitment towards this aspect of the work:

I think we have embraced the victim side: we have set up a service which should incorporate victims as well as offenders, and that is without question in all our approaches. But I think some staff would still feel that offenders were much more a priority - and to a certain extent I can understand their problems because we haven't got any guidance nationally about what that actually means. What does it mean to contact a victim every time a crime is committed - you know, in the way you work with offenders where there are national standards? So I think we've opened up systems to focus on victims but I think we struggle with what is best practice and there have been lots of problems arising that can't readily be answered.

(YOT manager)

Linked to this was a lack of clarity more generally about how to integrate restorative justice into practice. As one of the operational managers put it:

I would like to set up systems where that routinely happens: where it is part of routine intervention. But first perhaps we need to define exactly what restorative justice is within the YOT.

Like restorative justice, reparation to victims is a thread running through all of YOT work. Indeed it had now become a mandatory aspect of practice in the form of two performance measures to ensure that either direct or indirect reparation were provided. Performance measure 5 specifies that the use of restorative justice processes should be increased, and performance measure 6 promotes increases in the proportion of victims consulted and given the chance to participate in restorative processes, and increases in the proportion of victims who are satisfied with the outcome.

YOT staff were, in principle, in favour of arrangements for reparation by offenders, though increasingly this was perceived in the narrowest sense as 'apologising to the victim'. They did not lose sight, however, of the fact that, according to surveys, young offenders themselves are likely to have been victims of crime. Accordingly, they emphasised the desirability of reparation schemes that would be two-way in their payoffs - that is, reparation projects that would benefit the offenders as well as victims themselves. In particular, reparation projects were seen as learning opportunities for young offenders. Indeed this is a good example of how central policy and legislation may be modified by interpretations on the ground (Burnett and Appleton, 2004; Robinson and McNeill, 2004). This double-edged perspective on reparation was evident in a comment made by one YOT Manager when the community payback scheme was launched:

It's less about payback - more about making amends, and both sides of the contract need to come away with something. The community gets a service, the offender gets work experience or training... You do need a win-win outcome for this to work.

(Youth Justice Board, 2001b)

Reinforcing parental responsibility

The provision of specialised parenting programmes is an obvious way in which youth justice services are working to reinforce parental responsibility. Another instance was the work done with parents in the local YOI to include them as far as possible in the programme of work with their sons (see Chapter 8). But apart from these specific instances, it might be fair to conclude along with some previous youth justice workers that the reforms to youth justice resulted in less work being done with parents.

Few parenting orders were imposed, and practitioners working in the community acknowledged that there was more that they could be doing to address this objective. The move to case-management had served as a barrier because it encouraged an office-based style of working and a 'tick-box mentality' - what Pitts (2001) has referred to as 'karaoke'. If parenting had not been identified early on as problematic then it was a risk factor that was liable to be overlooked while attention was turned to other issues that had been ticked. One of the operational managers who had many years of experience in the former youth justice system explained in some detail how changes in practice had affected work with parents:

> Former youth justice worker: *As the YOT system has developed there has been much more emphasis on the young person fitting into our structures rather than them being seen much more holistically and including their parents. We were more aware in the old system of the expectation for parents to actively support their young person through whatever order they were on. That would enable us to assess whether parents were meeting their parental responsibility in relation to their young person. It would then inform us if the young person offended again; we would have evidence. I think now we have almost pulled the child out of the family and put him into our systems, but forgotten the parents. The only time the parents are involved is almost at the court stage, and if there happens to be a parenting order, which generally comes from education. So I think there is a lot more work that needs to be done on our structures and how we make sure parents are involved in the orders and at reviews so parents can give feedback about their concerns and how the young person is doing.*

> Interviewer: *In what ways were parents involved under the old system?*

> Former youth justice worker: *They were required to attend court and we attempted to make sure that they were there, and we then required them as part of the order to attend the initial planning meeting and then to attend all the reviews and no reviews would go ahead unless all the parents were there...Sometimes the most effective work can be done with the parents. Change the parents behaviour and you change the young person's behaviour. Our systems now are geared to us saying 'You have committed the offence therefore we will work with you'. Not 'You have committed the offence, we need to be working with you and your family'.*

Furthermore, previous specialised adolescent services in the social services department ceased to operate after the YOT was formed and so this was another way in which work with families had been reduced. However, the low volume of direct work with parents cannot only be attributed to such changes in working practices. Staff attitudes regarding what was possible were also relevant. Practitioners expressed doubts about their own ability to make a difference given the extent of problems presented by parents of young people in their caseloads. As one YOT worker said:

> *It sounds good but it's extremely difficult to do. Many parents with difficult wayward children are almost children themselves really, so - I totally agree that parental responsibility should be reinforced but in many cases, in my experience, you would be on a hiding to nothing.*

Others rejected the idea that their child's behaviour could be linked to their parenting ability. The explicit blaming of parents within reforms to youth justice, and implied by parenting orders, has made parenting a more sensitive topic. In some cases, work with parents was seen as a welfare issue requiring liaison between the YOT and social services, for example when a child has been abandoned by its parents: the division of responsibility between agencies needs to be explicitly defined.

Interventions to tackle the problems underlying offending

Thirty-three million pounds was devoted by the YJB to the development of interventions to prevent and reduce offending. Was the money well spent? The key questions of whether these specific interventions are tackling some of the causes of crime and are proving effective in reducing the likelihood of reoffending can only be fully answered over the longer term. Each of the national evaluation teams, appointed by the YJB to focus on specific categories of interventions - cognitive behavioural; restorative justice; mentoring; parenting; educational, training and employment; substance abuse - produced reports on the early outcomes. The task set for these national evaluation teams was thwarted by the absence of control groups and the limited availability of reconviction data (Wilcox, 2003). However, the reports of the evaluation teams provided useful information on the processes of setting up and implementing projects (e.g. Feilzer et al., 2002; Ghate and Ramella, 2002; Wilcox with Hoyle, 2002).

Evaluating the effectiveness of each specific project required separate considera-tion of various factors, including whether the project was:

- Fit for purpose and of sufficient quality.
- Correctly implemented and delivered.
- Targeting those for whom it was intended.
- Used by the target group.

It is not enough for a project to consist of a high quality programme of work that addresses a criminogenic factor; that is, a factor that is causally related to crime. The same project will not be effective if it is badly implemented. For example, it may be held in unsuitable premises or led by unqualified staff; or it may be offered to people who have less need for it, whilst the *intended* users do not get referred or drop out of the programme. The experiences of OYOT in setting up interventions exemplified factors which help projects to flourish and which cause others to stumble (see Chapter 7).

Beyond evaluation of the specific interventions set up, prior questions were

(a) whether the interventions were aimed at the most appropriate stage in criminal careers in order to be effective, and (b) whether the right age group has been targeted.

The question of where resources should best be concentrated - whether at the 'light end' when young people have just begun to offend (as is the case for final warnings and referral orders) or at the 'heavy end' (as is happening in the case of ISSPs and DTOs) - is a long-standing one. Opponents to the policy of early intervention aimed at 'nipping crime in the bud' argue that this could be counterproductive. Such a degree of intervention for young people, who at one time might have been dealt with by another caution or a conditional discharge, flies in the face of research findings of the last few decades which indicated that most young people stop offending more quickly if they are diverted from the criminal justice system (Goldson, 2000; Kemp et al., 2002).

While such arguments reject an early interventionist approach, aimed indiscriminately at all second-time (and some first-time) offenders, another view is that early intervention that simply targeted *predicted persistent* offenders would be appropriate. That is, instead of an injection of funding, such as was dedicated to the ISSP, it might be more appropriate to devote funding to working with those who are predicted to become persistent offenders *before* they reach that stage. Such a scheme might eliminate the need for an expensive and large-scale programme like ISSP if it helped reduce the number of persistent offenders reaching the stage of needing intensive supervision and surveillance.

An even more radical argument for the reallocation of funding calls into question whether the youth justice system has been targeting the right age group or whether the same sum might have been better spent on preventative initiatives for children younger that ten, even toddlers. Some of the young people dealt with are described by staff as 'so damaged and disaffected' by the time they are within the YOT's age range that the interventions, however good, cannot easily resolve those underlying problems. This highlights the need for preventative interventions at a very early age with those children whose family backgrounds put them into a high risk category. YOT work brought some staff into closer contact with younger offenders and 'brought home to them' how quickly even very young children become entrenched in a criminal lifestyle and the implications of this for youth justice services:

The other bit that this job has really taught me, is...the percentage of utterly damaged children of utterly damaged parents. And the concern for me on a much wider scale is what does society do with those most damaged families that are just going to go on repeating? The interventions can only touch the edge of the problem: you know, a parenting programme once a week and then they are going back to be beaten up by their son, or maybe husband. And that's the despairing bit for me and I think I suppose it has always been there: what do you do with people who are most disaffected? It brings home the importance of very early preventative interventions at a much younger age...It has led to me to think that it is the nought to three year olds we ought to be targeting...We are just the tip of the iceberg really. You need much more of joined-up services targeting that sort of really dysfunctional family and families that will be growing up with no sense of a stake in society. But that's much more global isn't it? It is a bit too much for the YOT.

(YOT practitioner)

The appropriateness of a diverse set of interventions differentiated by degree of involvement in criminal activity was recognised in the Audit Commission and seems to be a message that was taken up by the YJB:

Any strategy for tackling youth crime must consider how to address the behaviour of four different groups of young people. Targeting persistent offenders, to get them to change their behaviour, could have a significant effect on the overall level of youth crime. Young offenders who have yet to develop an entrenched pattern of offending must also be dealt with effectively; and first time offenders must also be discouraged from becoming more deeply involved in crime. Finally, young people at risk must be discouraged from getting involved in offending in the first place.

(Audit Commission, 1996: 13)

There is increasing research support for the value of interventions aimed, preventatively, at younger age groups (Schweinhart et al., 1993). Joined-up preventative work targeted at very young children of high-risk dysfunctional families is, of course, outside the range of youth offending teams and such preventative work had a lower profile when the YOTs were first launched. However, the later injection of YJB funding into YIPs, Splash projects and YISPs provided clear evidence of government and central support for this approach (see Box 4 in Chapter 5).

In addition to the specialist interventions and major programmes, the one-to-one work of practitioners is in itself a form of intervention that should not be underestimated. The new practice culture has resulted in more time with computers and paper and in discussion with colleagues and less time with young people and their families. The extended range of interventions has diluted the direct work with offenders and their families including opportunities for motivational work and pro-social modelling. This is key work which takes place in between specialist interventions and offending behaviour programmes, the importance of which should not be overlooked. Effective motivational work depends on the development of an effective practitioner-client relationship and the use of appropriate interpersonal skills by the practitioner (Young, 1999; Burnett, 2004). While core one-to-one work is important enough to be recognised as an intervention in its own right it is also crucial to the implementation of specialist interventions and accredited programmes. Without the appropriate skills, good programmes are likely to be less effective. YOT practitioners who welcomed evidence-based practice and the development of accredited programmes became aware that elements of previous practice were in danger of being overlooked. This was well articulated in the following interview extract:

I've just got a hankering after those old social work ideas about the quality of work that is being put in. Because you can do the same stuff in different ways:

you can do it in a very dull and boring pen and paper way and you can actually do it in a quite interesting and very focused way. That's the sort of qualitative stuff that ought to be looked at. Those communication skills are quite key. You can set up the most fantastic programme but without the right staff you are not going to get very good outcomes.   (Senior practitioner)

Setting up and delivering joined-up services

The basis by which YOTs were to achieve their aim was by corporate planning and delivery of interventions. The rhetoric of 'joined-up services' is the easy part. Achieving it requires the triumph of strategy and commitment over competing priorities and scarce resources. Our study revealed some of the difficulties in translating the rhetoric into reality. There were intimations of how rapid development can be achieved at the expense of detailed operational planning and how an agency might be galvanised into fulfilling a central, 'top-down' agenda while losing sight of its own.

Breadth versus depth

Less than a year after the YOTs became operational, the headline news in the YJB newsletter was that YOT partnerships were an 'unqualified success' (Pitkeathley, 2000) - though in the same issue the Chief Executive of the YJB more moderately assessed the progress of YOTs as 'up and running - but still with a long way to go' (Perfect, 2000). Thus, there was, at least, a sense of having arrived. As one of the operational managers in OYOT said: 'We have been successful in putting things together at high speed and making them roughly workable'. A skilled workforce was recruited, good relations with partner organisations were secured, bids for funding were successful as were competitive bids to pilot new initiatives, and one specialist project after another was quickly assembled. Initial scepticism was easily overpowered by enthusiasm. When the volume of work expanded and outgrew the workforce, there were periods where morale dropped, but the cynics were outnumbered by those who were 'willing to give it a bloody good go'. These were all positive omens.

But perhaps a new project or agency can be too quick for its own good in jumping through all the hoops, attracting yet more opportunities and then needing to expand before there has been sufficient time for the new arrangements to 'bed down'. The pathway YOT was a case in point. It made a habit of throwing up new shoots and being selected to pilot things. After the initial excitement that novelty imbues, there were niggling doubts followed by outright concerns that this venturesome approach had been at the expense of clarity and consolidation. There had not been time or sufficient staff to set up thorough systems and procedures and to secure the linkages between core practice and additional services and disposals. Staff attributed this tension between competing demands at least partly to the YJB, 'because of all the things they were throwing at us'. The YOT was seen as a victim of its own success. It is not always easy to disentangle strengths from weaknesses. Assessing both strengths and weaknesses, one staff member commented on the paradox that:

A strength is a recognition that there is still a lot to do but we must do it. A weakness might be that there is a tendency to look for the quickest ways to get there. So I think we may lose a lot in the stride for expediency.

The appointment of a deputy manager to focus on operational development was a turning point in providing the depth beneath the gloss on the surface.

Establishing and maintaining partnerships

Another way in which a multi-agency venture can be too successful for its own good is through the development of more partnerships than it can properly sustain. Partners bring burdens as well as gains and there may be just too many to tango with. Inevitably, countywide YOTs especially have faced a challenge to maintain links with partners across several district authorities. For example, the pathway YOT struggled to keep up contact with five community strategy groups, and with all schools in the county. The YOT manager acknowledged such blemishes on a generally good partnership record:

I'm aware that there are criticisms around about the YOT not being present at some community strategy meetings. We are weak in those areas, but there are five of them, and they have each all got their own information exchange protocols and protocols over anti-social behaviour orders. Without being cynical - because it is important that they are there - they are politically their own little authorities and they don't have to have anything to do with the county council if they don't want to. It's that political dimension which you wouldn't get in a unitary authority and it is very time-consuming. In the youth justice plan we would be criticised by the district authorities as not being very present. The other criticism would be from head teachers from schools, saying that the YOT doesn't come into their school. But how could you meet the needs of every school in the county when there is only one short-staffed YOT? I would hope they understand that.

(YOT manager)

Meeting the targets

The Youth Justice Board introduced performance measures (see Box 10) and made further funding dependent on meeting targets. Not surprisingly managers expressed objections. When the second YOT manager came into post, he conveyed some exasperation against the threat that funding would be withdrawn if targets were unmet. For example, the absence of exit strategies for projects would prompt the withholding of further funding, yet this might be in effect punishing a YOT for the poverty or unco-operativeness of its partner agencies:

All this business of eight and half per cent withholding seems to me to be a lot of nonsense actually. It is all very well to wave that as a stick but some YOTs may fail to achieve whatever it is they were being expected to achieve. And then it doesn't exactly help to achieve it in the following year if you take the funding away. But they are making every show that they are going to be checking really seriously; they are actually going to do it.

The target-driven approach to management has become even more pressured since May 2003 when the YJB began publishing performance tables on its website. It makes use of traffic light colours against each target to indicate which YOTs have performed well, satisfactorily or poorly. The YJB Head of Performance, when announcing the introduction of this system, anticipated that it would have 'a powerful effect in concentrating minds on how to address performance deficits' (Wright, 2003: 5).

The majority of young offenders are white males but another crucial aspect of service delivery is to build in provision for those who are in a minority: female and minority ethnic young offenders. The YJB requires YOTs to collate and analyse data by ethnicity and gender and, following the Race Relations (Amendment) Act 2000, it produced guidance and practical suggestions for 'establishing common framework to promote fairness for everyone with the youth justice system' (YJB, 2001d).

What kind of system is it?

Andrew Rutherford (1993) distinguished three clusters of values and beliefs, which he called 'working credos', that shape the daily work and careers of professionals working in criminal justice: one concerned with the punitive degradation of offenders, the second focusing on efficiency and management, and the third being a cluster of liberal and humane values. These 'ideal type' distinctions were subsequently adapted by Cavadino and Dignan to categorise criminal justice strategies:

Strategy A: Punitive
...involve[s] making criminal justice harsher and more punitive at every stage and in every respect. [It] embodies an 'exclusionary' approach to offenders, tending to reject them as members of the community.

Strategy B: Managerialist
...seeks to apply administrative and bureaucratic mechanisms to criminal justice in an attempt to make the system as smooth running and cost-effective as possible.

Strategy C: Humanitarian
...seeks to protect and uphold the human rights of offenders, victims and potential victims of crime. It seeks to minimise punishment and to ensure fairness and humane treatment within the community and reintegrate them as law-abiding citizens into the criminal justice system.

(Cavadino and Dignan, 2002: 5-6)

The new youth justice has many critics. It has been impugned for blaming young people and their parents for youth crime while doing too little to tackle child poverty and neighbourhood factors (Pitts, 2000; 2003; Gelsthorpe, 2000; Muncie, 2000); for replacing effective diversionary strategies with punitive measures which are an infringement of children's rights (Goldson, 2000); for pandering to punitive populism; and misguidedly pursuing an imagined past where young people could be made to behave by commonsensical use of discipline (Pitts, 2000). The emphasis on punishment is criticised as failing to take account of the immaturity of young people and the wider structural causes of crime (Haines, 2000).

The system also has its champions, though generally they are among YJB staff and government officials. In our view, the most outspoken assessments of the shifts in youth justice have been over-extreme in one direction or another (Burnett and Appleton, 2004) and can be dichotomised into what Pearson et al. (1992) distinguished as 'conspiratorial' versus 'benevolent' perspectives. In between these polar positions, a more moderate appraisal is that, rather than being purely concerned with punishment and pandering to the public opinion, the changes may have been at least equally about saving money (Cavadino and Dignan, 2002; Smith, 2000). As suggested by Faulkner (2001: 219):

The Labour Government undoubtedly found the youth justice system in a state of administrative confusion and neglect when it entered office in May 1997, with justified and well documented complaints about delays, waste of time and money, and ineffectiveness in terms of the impact it was making on young people who became involved with it.

The damning review of the Audit Commission in 1996 found that public services were spending around £1 billion a year in processing and dealing with youth crime while only 3 per cent of offences committed by young people were leading to formal proceedings. As much as anything therefore, the new arrangements were intended to shake-up a very inefficient and economically wasteful system.

It cannot be denied, however, that the new policy included 'punishment' and that a rise in custodial sentences for young people was one of the unfortunate consequences. This could have been anticipated given that the new system would be:

- Bringing more young people into the criminal justice system at an earlier stage.
- Dealing with each offence more quickly and so exhausting the community options more quickly.
- Promoting DTOs as educational and linked with community interventions.

However, the impression to be gained from some critics is that the legislation was intended to be repressive and coercive, and resulted in lots of children being flung into prison because magistrates, with the government's blessing, were intent on inflicting pain and on being 'nasty to children' (Jones, 1996).

A less cynical reading of official documentation suggests that the bark of the new legislation was intended to be more fierce than its bite. The White Paper mentioned that there is no conflict between welfare and preventing offending:

Children need protection as appropriate from the full rigour of criminal law. Under the UN Convention on the Rights of the Child and the European Convention on Human Rights, the United Kingdom is committed to protecting the welfare of children and young people who come into contact with the criminal justice process. The Government does not accept that there is any conflict between protecting the welfare of a young offender and preventing that individual from offending again. Preventing offending promotes the welfare of the individual young offender and protects the public.

(Home Office, 1997: section 2.2)

Critics have regarded this statement as disingenuous, but the framework document for the Crime and Disorder Act only mentioned 'punishment' twice whereas the concept of 'welfare' appeared much more frequently, and the overall message was more constructive than punitive:

The response to a child or young person's offending needs to be constructive and appropriate. Whether intervention following an admission of guilt or conviction is community-based or a custodial sentence, the emphasis should be on taking effective action to prevent further offending and on carrying out the groundwork needed to allow the child or young person to be effectively re-integrated into the community and to stay away from further crime.

(Home Office, 1998: section 7)

Equally, the Youth Justice Board might be accused of being over zealous in its self-proclaimed success but it is hard to find evidence of a punitive approach. The concept of 'punishment' rarely features in YJB literature, and when it does it is linked to rehabilitation and reparation. In an article by the then YJB Chair, Lord Warner linked the Board's philosophy of punishment to its educational and rehabilitative role, and rejected punishment as retribution (Warner, 2003). The Board's position on custody which he put forward was that it is appropriate for those who are a danger to the public and to themselves. He expressed regret that politicians and the press sometimes read the public's disapproval of crime as a demand for severe punishment, and argued that punishment should consist of demands and loss of privileges but should also be constructive, providing opportunities to learn and change. His comparison of this to 'good parenting' was somewhat undermined by inappropriate use of the 'sticks and carrots' metaphor. Overall, his argument was in line with the principle in *No More Excuses* that the purpose of disposals and sentences should be to prevent reoffending, which is 'in the best interests of the young person' as well as being in the best interest of the public (Home Office, 1997c: para. 2.3).

This balance between imposing penalties and providing opportunities has been evident in all the Youth Justice Board literature and is consistent with the findings of the present research. While we regard the stories of consummate success running through the YJB newsletter with some scepticism, the detailed case-study we carried out in one county over a two-year period did not substantiate portrayals of the system as overly punitive and unjust. Indeed, the overwhelming impression was that the new legislation and the resulting joined-up services had increased the range of help and opportunities extended to young people. It was much closer to the 'humanitarian system' in Cavadino and Dignan's categorisation. If the official procedures, sentences and interventions really were intended as punitive measures then most of the youth justice workforce have misguidedly steered them away from punishment and towards opportunities for restorative justice and social inclusion. In all of our discussions with the diverse professionals involved in this joined-up enterprise none of them referred explicitly to 'punishment' as an objective of their contribution - apart from a few magistrates and, then, only in an educational rather than retributive sense (see Duff, 2002). Such arguments defending the communicative role of punishing juveniles is a long way from approving the use of imprisonment for them. No-one was holding up a banner for putting young people behind bars. The previous Chief Inspector's view (Ramsbotham, 2001) that prison is no place for children, even though a secure place is sometimes necessary, was a view expressed by many participants in the youth justice system.

Searching for a positive side to New Labour's criminal justice policies, Gelsthorpe (2002: 62) noted that:

> *The seed of hope for a return to issues of social justice lie in the fact that the Social Exclusion Unit and the Community Development Foundation have created programmes to facilitate greater access for young people in the employment market and have encouraged social improvement in socially deprived areas.*

The educational, training and employment projects developed as part of joined-up youth justice have been in line with, and complementary to, such a policy of inclusion. In this case-study, for example, certainly the intention and often the achievement of partnership projects covered a wide range of constructive interventions that were not remotely punitive and which were nearly always provided on a voluntary basis. For example, projects were set-up to:

- Help young people who had difficulty in reading and writing to improve these skills.
- Enable non-attending or excluded children back into school.
- Better prepare school leavers for the job market.
- Offer supportive friendship and mentoring.
- Restore the bonds between parents and their children.
- Facilitate training and educational opportunities.
- Give specialist support to young drug abusers.
- Provide a 'safety-net' for homeless or profoundly troubled youngsters.

But, most of all, it was the obvious value base of practitioners - whether senior management or front-line staff - that convinced us that, even in this era of explicit 'correctionalism', the system continues to be humanitarian and welfare-orientated. Reviewing the changes to youth justice on the eve of the new reforms, Gelsthorpe criticised the policies as misconceived but commented that the practitioner movement of the 1980s, in which practitioners resisted a 'crime control' approach and focussed on diverting young people away from formal intrusive and custodial measures, gave hope of 'wise practice on the ground'(2002: 62). Following recent studies of probation practice in both England and Wales, and in Scotland, Robinson and McNeill (2003) concluded that despite transitions in 'official' statements of objectives, the front-line staff were 'far from being the passive vessels of "official" discourses'. Rather, they tended to reframe traditional practice so that it would fit with policy statements.

Similarly, in this case-study of reformed youth justice services, we found that traditional methods and values were regularly reasserted as necessary and important - not least by staff who welcomed the new focus on crime reduction and evidence-based practice (Burnett and Appleton, 2004). The moves in the National Probation Service towards enforcement of involuntary attendance of accredited programmes have not yet been paralleled in the youth justice system. Those engaged in the supervision of young people adapted well to using information technology and more systematic case-management but they continued to do what in former days was called 'social work'. Faced with the chaotic lives and often desperate social circumstances of their young charges, the provision of a supportive relationship and attention to welfare needs were the assumed essentials of the job.

CHAPTER 10

A Model to Follow: Avoiding the Pitfalls and Improving the Potential

The youth justice system brought in by New Labour on the eve of the new century has been favourably described as, 'a bold innovation that deserves to succeed' (Faulkner, 2001: 219) but, as we discussed in Chapter 9, there have been various doomsayers, and criminologists are prominent amongst them. Indeed, several publications are polemical critiques of the system - notably, John Pitts's *The New Politics of Youth Crime* (2003) and Roger Smith's *Youth Justice, Ideas, Policy, Practice* (2003) - and the journal *Youth Justice* has, so far, featured articles which are essentially opposed to the underlying philosophy and policies.

Yet the 'new youth justice' in England and Wales has been hailed as a model to follow. An identical approach is being set up in New Zealand, and now Scotland is following suit. Those in favour of our new youth justice provisions have hailed it as an example of inter-agency, joined-up working that should be adopted more widely. More cautious commentators have been watching to see how well the system delivers its promises and overcomes its weaknesses. Some of its features - inter-agency teamwork; oversight by a non-government body; the application of restorative justice approaches to include victims and to involve the community - have been commended as appropriate for other areas of the criminal justice system (Faulkner, 2001). It has been noted that the partnership arrangements involved are far more comprehensive than those previously applied within the criminal justice system and that the arrangements may hold lessons for adult community penalties (Bottoms et al., 2001). More generally, the reformed youth justice system exemplifies 'joined-up' services that are evolving in many quarters and which are increasingly regarded as essential for contemporary public services. For example, see the report of the Performance and Innovation Unit, *Wiring it Up* (PIU, 2000), the White Paper *Justice for All* (Home Office, 2002b) and the Green Paper *Every Child Matters* (Home Office, 2003).

While there may not yet be sufficient reason to rejoice in our new co-operative model of youth justice; we can at least acknowledge the positive elements of New Labour's systemic managerialism (Newburn, 2002). It has been suggested by David Smith, professor of social work at Lancaster University, that we have perhaps been witnessing a return to the principled pragmatism and co-operation that were characteristic of the corporatist approach promoted by the Home Office during the late 80's and early 90's, prior to the populist agenda of home secretary, Michael Howard. Smith suggests that emphasis on partnership, a common aim, and shared responsibility in New Labour's youth justice policies, were an attempt to get back to the greater efficiency and effectiveness of the period prior to 1993 after which government interest in a partnership approach seemed to wane and custody rates began to rise (Smith, 2001).

Our purpose in this volume has been neither to condemn nor to defend the changes, but to provide a picture of how the reforms have worked out in practice during the early years of implementation. In doing so, we have concentrated on reporting findings of relevance to the efforts of all those involved in delivering youth justice services. In keeping with this spirit of constructive pragmatism, this chapter will draw together key learning points and recommendations. Throughout the previous chapters we have pointed to emerging benefits of the new arrangements as well as problems arising. We bring them together here in order to take stock of the main difficulties that have been overcome or that remain as challenges and to highlight constructive ways of moving forward.

Developing a multi-agency organisation

The formation of a multi-agency partnership to tackle important social issues and to deliver major changes in policy or legislation is, inevitably, a very challenging undertaking. The experience of OYOT indicates that, to succeed, such a radical reorganisation requires first class leadership, committed and competent staff and a spirit of optimism. The leadership provided the inspiration, direction and influence which led to funding and the formation of partnerships. The workforce provided the effort and skills to 'make it happen'.

The development of this multi-agency initiative benefited from changes in management: first the creation of the post of deputy manager and then serendipitous change of manager at the top. While the early departure of the first manager seemed a misfortune at the time, it proved advantageous because the different management styles complemented the successive stages of growth. There seems to have been an object lesson here. New organisations benefit from a founding manager with vision and energy to set up an agency from its conception and to assemble all the relevant parts. They then further thrive via a management style focused on fortifying and consolidating the early foundations and then sustaining towards maturity.

It may seem obvious that a multi-agency initiative that involves new services and reorganisation of existing services requires a multi-agency budget. Yet funding arrangements introduced by the Youth Justice Board focused attention on specialised projects and encouraged short-term, one-sided arrangements while the start-up funds were still flowing. The acquisition of an adequate pooled budget for the development of a multi-agency service is more likely to be achieved when each agency sees the service as co-ordinated with the plans of their own agency.

The model steering group for a multi-agency initiative is formed by top-level managers who can exercise budgetary control in their own agency and who will be involved in the planning of the service. OYOT began with such a steering group and the first manager encouraged a sense of shared ownership of the YOT's agenda and its services. The steering group, however, lapsed into being less strategic and the pooled budget was meagre. Insufficient regard was given to the need for future funding from partner agencies. A multi-agency partnership requires a *strategic* steering group not only at the time of its formation but on a continuing basis to ensure an adequate budget for forward planning, and to promote a sense of shared ownership and responsibility.

The publicity drive of the YJB encouraged inflated claims and a focus on positive interpretations perhaps at the expense of attention to detail and realism. A pathway YOT has some obligation to share its experiences, but it sometimes seemed that it was part of a race to claim success before there was any evidence of it and irrespective of underlying problems. Such publicity is inimical to 'evidence-based practice' which is also a promoted feature of the new youth justice.

The setting up of YOT services turned out to be a 'hell for leather' development in which the provision of resources for specialised interventions outpaced the provision of resources for central practice. Attention to the more glamorous new approaches can carry a price. While more innovative work was taken on and the volume of work expanded, core practice lacked basic resources such as suitable interviewing rooms, administrative systems and sufficient staff. In a partnership arena that offers opportunities to expand and develop specialist services, there is a balance to strike between developing those additional initiatives and nurturing and resourcing the essential, central services to ensure their quality.

Key learning points

*   A successful multi-agency partnership requires first class leadership, committed and competent staff and a spirit of optimism.
*   The early development of a complex organisation may benefit greatly from staged changes in leadership, from founding manager to consolidating manager, in order to benefit from appropriate skills at the appropriate time.
*   The acquisition of an adequate pooled budget for the development of a multi-agency service is more likely to be achieved when each agency sees the service as co-ordinated with the plans of their own agency.
*   A multi-agency partnership requires a *strategic* steering group to ensure an adequate budget for forward planning, and to promote a sense of shared ownership and responsibility.
*   New partnership initiatives that are centrally led should resist pressure to publicise outcomes and to trumpet success before evidence has been accumulated and before detailed systems and operations have been secured.
*   In a partnership arena that offers opportunities to expand and develop specialist services, there is balance to strike between developing those additional initiatives and nurturing and resourcing the essential, central services to ensure their quality.

The core services

The opportunity to work alongside practitioners from various agencies proved valuable but the multi-professional environment became a melting pot because eventually staff all tended to take on the mantle of being a 'YOT worker'. Staff from different backgrounds felt cut off from their parent agencies and were concerned that returning after secondment would be difficult, and also that opportunities to take advantage of their agency link were diminishing. There should be opportunities for them to return to their parent agencies to update and refresh their specialisms. To keep the distinctions between police, probation, social services, education and health workers alive, there needs to be a frequent influx of staff seconded from these agencies. At the same time, there should be opportunities for some staff to remain in the inter-agency team on a more permanent basis so that there is an accumulation of wisdom.

An unintended consequence of working in an inter-agency setting may be that people swap the role for which they are best qualified for another that is outside their own range of skills and experience. There were various instances of this occurring; for example, mental health specialists were faced with welfare issues when home-visiting, and mentors got involved attending case conferences. YOT practitioners, on the other hand, felt that the need to spend extra time in the office carrying out case-management tasks too frequently kept them away from such roles. The boundaries to be maintained between roles and legitimate cross-over of roles should be kept under review.

The formation of multi-agency services, and reorganisation more generally, might give rise to gaps in provision as a result of some merging and exchange of roles. Longer serving practitioners observed that family support services and welfare provision for adolescents, previously the concern of social services, were neglected as a result of the focus on offending behaviour and the office based case-management approach. Comparisons of services before and after extensive reorganisation should be made to guard against the possibility of 'collateral damage' and to fill any holes that emerge.

A service that covers a large geographical area will inevitably face the tensions between what is good for the service as a whole and differing local requirements. Also, it is difficult for team members based in a local community to avoid adopting a local identity that distinguishes them from others based elsewhere. Recent developments in operational management led to progress in eliminating regional competitiveness and in promoting consistency and the sharing of best practice. However, there remained some tendency for regionally based staff to 'do their own thing' in adapting to local circumstances and opportunities. Variation in the delivery of final warnings is an example. It should be the aim of all the YOT's managers to ensure that uniformity and consistency are achieved wherever possible and to inculcate a countywide team spirit that cuts across the local divide.

Communication within each regional unit was good. However, there was scope for greater communication and co-ordination across the YOT and also between YOT officers and project staff. More bridges need to be built in the form of support networks and regular meetings. Good systems developed in one unit should be shared with others.

The new procedures and orders - in particular, final warnings and referral orders - required vast amounts of work to set up and administer followed by the delivery of interventions. There were often delays in getting started. It defeats the object of the disposals, and of fast tracking, if the young person is left hanging-on without anything happening, giving the impression that such orders exist only in theory and are meaningless. For the new legislation and services to work in practice, it is obviously crucial to ensure there are enough staff to administer them and for delays to be avoided, in accordance with national standards, to ensure that words are translated into action and disposals are demonstrably what they purport to be.

The case-management model that was adopted was not a pure model, but that may have been its saving grace. Staff continued to form a casework relationship with young people for whom they were the keyworker even though proportionally more of their work was desk-based and office-based. While emphasis on a one-to-one casework relationship has fallen out of favour following the highly publicised reviews of 'what works' to reduce offending, good assessment and effective supervision can only be achieved via the establishment of a close working relationship with the young person concerned. The needs of young people for a consistent relationship with a stable youth justice official should be balanced with the use of interventions to address criminogenic factors. In order for YOT practitioners to play their part in 'confronting offenders with the consequences of their behaviour', the direct work they do with young people remains important.

It is ironic that, while specialist projects such as the mentor system and the family-based approach of the mental health team are inheriting some aspects of traditional casework, these roles were being reduced if not lost in core practice. It would be odd if the case-management approach led practitioners away from this most fundamental element of youth work. If the need that young people have for a consistent relationship is not met by practitioners there may be a tendency for it to be pushed elsewhere, perhaps less appropriately.

A recurring theme during the evaluation of projects and core practice is that of motivation. Not surprisingly, the best results are gained when young people - and their carers in the case of parenting work - are motivated to take up and engage with interventions. The whole YOT enterprise is haunted by the spectre of staff being stood-up or shrugged off by disinterested adolescents. In getting young people to benefit from projects, motivation is no less relevant when attendance is a mandatory requirement of an order. Motivational interviewing is therefore a valuable skill for both practitioners and project staff to acquire. Specialist training in motivational interviewing should be provided.

Several grand ideas were claimed as features of all the YOT's work, notably restorative justice and education inclusion, yet these tended to be manifest in only small pockets of the YOT's work rather than applied cohesively across the service. More should be done to ensure that these high sounding principles are translated into consistent countywide practices to which all staff contribute. For example, there was a lack of clarity about whose role it is to work with victims and what that means in practice. Even though work was in progress to develop a victim policy and a good start has been made in securing victim participation, this work has not been systematically connected across different aspects of service. The victim liaison team was used in a patchy way and the reparation scheme was mainly directed at referral orders while not being linked in with final warnings. There was an assumption that victims were 'satisfied' with the way they were included even though there was little evidence to back this up. Arrangements for victim contact and victim participation require a co-ordinated countywide approach. Likewise, a strategic approach is needed to integrate restorative justice practices into the various disposals and services.

The national reconviction rates following final warnings have been presented as indicating the success of an interventionist approach. However, as discussed in Chapter 9, these data are contentious and they are contrary to earlier research findings in which diversion rather than intervention appeared to be the most effective way of dealing with initial offending behaviour. Further research and more time will be needed to investigate these contradictory findings. Labelling effects, association with others who are more criminalised, the rapid graduation though a hierarchy of sentences to a level reserved for the hardened offender may each be unintended consequences of reforms which make insufficient allowance for individual differences. The pervasive use of rehabilitative interventions for young people who have very few or no previous convictions is driven by the need to meet central targets. Rigorous assessment procedures, rather than pressure to meet performance targets, should be used to determine which interventions, if any, are appropriate.

Key learning points

- To maintain the benefits of multi-agency services, practitioners need opportunities to update their specialist knowledge and there should be a regular influx of new staff seconded from the contributing agencies.
- At the same time, there should be opportunities for some staff to remain in the multi-agency team on a more permanent basis so that there is an accumulation of wisdom.
- The boundaries to be maintained between roles and legitimate exchange of roles should be kept under review.
- Comparisons of services before and after extensive reorganisation should be made to guard against the possibility of 'collateral damage' and to fill any holes that emerge.
- Discussion forums and support networks should be provided to inculcate a team spirit that overrides any geographical divisions, and to promote consistency of practice.
- For the new legislation and services to work in practice it is obviously crucial to ensure there are enough staff to administer them.
- In order for YOT practitioners to play their part in 'confronting offenders with the consequences of their behaviour', the direct work they do with young people to engage their motivation and to provide a consistent relationship remains a fundamental element of youth work.
- Young offenders will respond better to interventions if they have positive as well as negative reasons for getting involved and keeping up attendance. Good preparatory work is critical. Specialist training in motivational interviewing should be provided for both practitioners and project staff.
- More should be done to ensure that the principles of 'restorative justice' and 'education inclusion' are translated into consistent countywide practices to which

all staff contribute. Arrangements for victim contact and victim participation require a co-ordinated countywide approach. Likewise, a strategic approach is needed to integrate restorative justice practices into the various disposals and services.

- Rigorous assessment procedures, rather than pressure to meet performance targets, should be used to determine which interventions, if any, are appropriate.

Specialist projects

The best results were obtained when a project was both (a) clearly seen to be addressing a need frequently presented by YOT cases - such as mental health problems or lack of qualifications to enter the job market - and (b) proactive in seeking contact with YOT staff and in discussing mutual clients. For a partnership contract to work, both parties needed to share some confidence that the arrangements would be mutually satisfactory or, at least, that the risks would be shared (Harrison et al., 2003).

Some of the projects were underused by YOT staff. Projects need a clear referral policy and to be made visible to practitioners on a regular basis. The project staff had to devote time to building good relations rather than relying on the content of the programme to sell itself. The main stumbling block for projects that were discontinued was a lack of communication both at senior and practitioner level.

There was occasional uncertainty or confusion about the existence or identity of certain projects contributing to youth justice services. This occurred when practitioners or potential users did not recognise the name of a project, or when they knew the name but had been misled by it. It may seem obvious, but in an era when new projects and initiatives pop up almost daily in the public sector, many of them short-lived and with overlapping purposes, it is important that they are given relevant and memorable names.

A proportion of the YOT's clients did not meet the criteria for referral to services that were already available. It was therefore necessary to develop services that were more geared to young people who would otherwise 'fall through the net'. Some projects could have done more to either target or accommodate people who are hard to reach. This study showed that projects intended to serve a multi-agency endeavour can flourish even though they are scarcely catering for the consumers of one or more of the partner services.

Key learning points

- Partnership contracts require detailed planning and, before proceeding, all parties should have confidence that the terms offer good prospects of being mutually beneficial.
- Projects should have realistic and clear eligibility criteria.
- They should not be too stringent in imposing selection criteria lest they end up discriminating against some of the very people they are designed to serve.
- Services with a share in using multi-user projects should ensure that a sufficient number of places are ring-fenced for their own referrals - though, equally, they

should make every effort to take up those reserved places so that they are not wasted.

- However good the project, it should not be assumed that it will 'sell itself' because busy professionals are likely to have their attention focussed elsewhere. Project staff should therefore be proactive in promoting the service, for example, by providing seminars and periodically attending staff meetings.
- Agencies using a project also have a responsibility to find out all they need to know about the project in order to make full and appropriate use of it. Managers should issue systematic referral policies to eliminate the likelihood of referrals being made on an arbitrary or subjective basis.
- Giving prospective participants on projects a chance to meet project facilitators in advance of referral is a good way to dispel worries, provide information and engage interest in attending. In such meetings motivational material can be used (e.g. leaflets; computerised assessment procedures).
- The provision of transport - and child-minding support in some cases - would no doubt result in additional referrals to projects and increased attendance.
- Written material used in programmes should be kept as simple as possible and should be supplemented by illustrations and verbal explanation so that anyone with literacy difficulties can still participate. Related to this, a classroom atmosphere should be avoided.
- All projects should have integrated monitoring and evaluation systems to enable the systematic collection of (a) participants' satisfaction with the project and (b) outcome information to test whether the project is achieving its objectives.
- Project staff should be provided with as much information as possible about the young people referred to them. Assessment records and written reports may be the quickest and most effective way of getting such information to them. Equally, the referring practitioner should be kept fully informed by project staff about the participants' progress on a project, and copies of project records may be the fastest way of achieving this. More time-consuming discussions could then be the 'icing on the cake'.

Concluding note

It has been suggested that the political and strategic responsibility for youth justice which previously belonged to local authorities has now been taken over by central government: while the YJB 'steers' the administration of youth justice, local authorities do the 'rowing' (Crawford, 1997; Pitts, 2000). Those involved in forging the local arrangements and putting together the youth justice plan for their region are likely to have a different perspective on their own contribution. The first few years of developing and strengthening local youth justice services have been creative and enterprising - as may be confirmed by any perusal of youth justice plans from various areas. There has been much evidence of local 'vision' and contributors have been creatively steering as well as paddling. The wide range of services and projects involved and the development of local youth justice plans has allowed considerable scope for variability during the stage of early development. Even so, the blueprint for the formative period was centrally imposed, and the linking of funding to achievement of targets places YOTs under considerable pressure. When a method of grading and then publishing the performance of YOTs was introduced by the YJB it was suggested that this would concentrate minds on addressing performance deficits (Wright, 2003). The challenge for all those involved will be to avoid being so focused on targets that they lose sight of the bigger picture, and to remain open to ways in which they can improve and reinforce the best elements of the emergent system.

References

Allen, C., Crow, I. and Cavadino, M. (2000) *Evaluation of the Youth Court Demonstration Project*. Home Office Research Study 214. London: Research, Development and Statistics Directorate.

Audit Commission (1996) *Misspent Youth: Young People and Crime*. London: Audit Commission.

Bailey, R. and Williams, B. (2000) *Inter-agency Partnerships in Youth Justice: Implementing the Crime and Disorder Act 1998*. Sheffield: University of Sheffield Joint Unit for Social Service Research.

Baker, K. (2004) Is *Asset* Really an Asset? Assessment of Young Offenders, in Practice, in Burnett, R. and Roberts, C. (eds.) *Evidence-Based Practice in Probation and Youth Justice*. Cullompton: Willan.

Bateman, T. (2001) Custodial Sentencing of Children: Prospects for Reversing the Tide. *Youth Justice*. 1: 1, 28-39.

Blair, T. (2003) Re-offending on the Decrease: Reversing the Trends and Breaking the Links. *Youth Justice Board News*. 17: 6-7.

Bottoms, A., Gelsthorpe, L. and Rex, S. (eds.) (2001) Introduction: The Contemporary Scene for Community Penalties, in Bottoms, A., Gelsthorpe, L. and Rex, S. (eds.) *Community Penalties: Change and Challenge*. Cullompton: Willan.

Braithwaite, J. (1989) *Crime, Shame and Re-integration*. Cambridge: Cambridge University Press.

Burnett, R. (1996) *Fitting Supervision to Offenders: Assessment and Allocation Decisions in the Probation Service*. Home Office Research Study 153. London: Home Office.

Burnett, R. (2004) One-to-one Ways of Promoting Desistance: In Search of an Evidence-Base, in Burnett, R. and Roberts, C. (eds.) *Evidence-Based Practice in Probation and Youth Justice*. Cullompton: Willan.

Burnett, R. and Appleton, C. (2004) Joined-up Services to Tackle Youth Crime: A Case-Study in England. *British Journal of Criminology*. 44: 1.

Cavadino, M. and Dignan, J. (2002) *The Penal System: An Introduction*. 3rd edn. London: Sage.

Chapman, T. and Hough, M. (1998) *Evidence Based Practice: A Guide to Effective Practice*. London: Home Office.

Clarke, A. (1999) *Evaluation Research: An Introduction to Principles, Methods and Practice*. London: Sage.

Cohen, S. (1983) *Folk Devils and Moral Panics*. London: Martin Robertson.

Cohen, S. (1985) *Visions of Social Control*. London: Polity Press.

Crawford, A. (1997) *The Local Governance of Crime: Appeals to Community and Partnerships*. Oxford: Clarendon Press.

Crawford, A. and Newburn, T. (2002) Recent Developments in Restorative Justice for Young People in England and Wales: Community Participation and Representation. *British Journal of Criminology*. 42: 476-95.

Crawford, A. and Newburn, T. (2003) *Youth Offending and Restorative Justice: Implementing Reform in Youth Justice*. Cullompton: Willan.

Cusick, J., Lindfield, S. and Coleman, J. (2000) *Working with Parents in the Youth Justice*

Context. Brighton: Trust for the Study of Adolescence.

Dewhurst, L. (2000) *Inhabiting the Margins: Elmore Team Good Practice Report.* London: National Homeless Alliance.

Drakeford, M. (2001) Children, Rights and Welfare: Towards a New Synthesis. *Youth Justice.* 1: 1, 40-4.

Duff, A. (2002) Punishing the Young, in Weijers, I. and Duff, A. (eds.) *Punishing Juveniles: Principle and Critique.* Oxford: Hart.

Eadie, T. and Canton, R. (2002) Practising in the Context of Ambivalence: The Challenge for Youth Justice Workers. *Youth Justice.* 2: 1, 14-26.

Estrada, F. (1999) Juvenile Trends in Post-war Europe. *European Journal on Criminal Policy and Research.* 7: 23-42.

Farrington, D. (1992) Trends in English Juvenile Delinquency and Their Explanation. *International Journal of Comparative and Applied Criminal Justice.* 16: 2, 151-63.

Farrington, D. (1996) *Understanding and Preventing Youth Crime.* Social Policy Research Findings, 93. York: Joseph Rowntree Foundation.

Faulkner, D. (2001) *Crime, State and Citizen: A Field Full of Folk.* Winchester: Waterside Press.

Feilzer, M. with Appleton, C., Roberts, C. and Hoyle, C. (2002) *Cognitive Behavioural Projects in Youth Justice: Final Report to the Youth Justice Board from the National Evaluation Team.* Oxford: Centre for Criminological Research.

Fionda, J. (1999) New Labour, Old Hat: Youth Justice and the Crime and Disorder Act 1998. *Criminal Law Review.* Jan. 36-47.

Flood-Page, C., Campbell, S., Harrington, V., et al. (2000) *Youth Crime: Findings from the 1998/99 Youth Lifestyles Survey.* Home Office Research Study 209. London: Home Office Research, Development and Statistics Directorate.

Fransham, M. (2002) *Promoting Positive Outcomes for Young People in Custody: HMYOI Huntercombe and Oxfordshire YOT.* MSc dissertation, Department of Applied Social Studies, University of Oxford.

Fullwood, C. and Powell, H. (2004) in Burnett, R. and Roberts, C. (eds.) *Evidence-Based Practice in Probation and Youth Justice.* Cullompton: Willan.

Garland, D. (2001) *The Culture of Control.* Oxford: University of Oxford.

Gelsthorpe, L. (2002) Recent Changes in Youth Policy in England and Wales, in Weijers, I. and Duff, A. (eds.) *Punishing Juveniles: Principle and Critique.* Oxford: Hart.

Ghate, D. and Ramella, M. (2002) *Positive Parenting: The National Evaluation of the Youth Justice Board's Parenting Programme.* London: Youth Justice Board.

Goldson, B. (ed.) (2000) *The New Youth Justice*, Lyme Regis: Russell House Publishing.

Goldson, B. (2000)'Wither Diversion? Interventionism and the New Youth Justice, in Goldson, B. (ed.) *The New Youth Justice.* Lyme Regis: Russell House Publishing.

Graham, J. and Bowling, B. (1995) *Young People and Crime.* Home Office Research Study 145, London: Home Office.

Haines, K. and Drakeford, M. (1998) *Young People and Youth Justice.* Basingstoke: Macmillan.

Haines, K. (2000) Referral Orders and Youth Offender Panels: Restorative Approaches and the New Youth Justice, in Goldson, B. (ed.) *The New Youth Justice.* Lyme Regis: Russell House Publishing.

Hancock, S. (2000) Practical Implications of the Crime and Disorder Act for Youth Offending Teams: A Youth Offending Team's Perspective, in Pickford, J. (ed.) *Youth Justice: Theory and Practice.* London: Cavendish.

Harrison, R., Mann, G., Murphy, M., et al. (2003) *Partnership Made Painless.* Lyme Regis: Russell House Publishing.

Hazel, N., Hagell, A., Liddle, M., et al. (2002) *Detention and Training: Assessment of the Detention and Training Order and its Impact on the Secure Estate across England and Wales.* London: Youth Justice Board.

Hedderman, C. and Williams, C. (2001) *Making Partnerships Work: Emerging Findings from the Reducing Burglary Initiative.* Policing and Reducing Crime Unit. London: Home Office.

Henggeler, S.W., Schoenwald, S., Borduin, C., et al. (1998) *Multi-systemic Treatment of Anti-social Behavior.* New York: Guildford Press.

Hine, J. and Celnick, A. (2001) *A One Year Reconviction Study of Final Warnings.* Sheffield: University of Sheffield.

HMIP (1997) *Young Prisoners: A Thematic Review by HM Chief Inspector of Prisons for England and Wales.* London: Her Majesty's Inspectorate of Prisons.

HMIP (2001) *Report on a Full Announced Inspection of HM Young Offenders Institution Huntercombe, 15 to 19 October 2001.* London: Her Majesty's Inspectorate of Prisons.

Holdaway, S., Davidson, N., Dignan, J., et al. (2001) *New Strategies to Address Youth Offending: The National Evaluation of The Pilot Youth Offending Teams.* London: Home Office Research, Development and Statistics Directorate.

Holt, P. (2000) *Case Management: Context for Supervision: A Review of Research on Models of Case Management.* Community and Criminal Justice Monograph 2. Leicester: De Montfort University.

Home Office (1990) *The Cautioning of Offenders.* Circular 59/1990. London: HMSO.

Home Office (1994) *The Criminal Histories of Those Cautioned in 1985, 1988 and 1991.* London: Home Office.

Home Office (1995) *Digest 3: Information on the Criminal Justice System in England and Wales.* London: Home Office Research and Statistics Department.

Home Office (1997a) *A New National and Local Focus on Youth Crime: A Consultation Paper.* Oct.

Home Office (1997b) *Youth Justice: the Statutory Principal Aim of Preventing Offending by Children and Young People.* London: Home Office.

Home Office (1997c) *No More Excuses: A New Approach to Tackling Youth Crime in England and Wales.* Cmd. 3809. London: HMSO.

Home Office (1998) *Youth Justice: Preventing Offending, Framework Document,* http://www.homeoffice.gov.uk/cdact/youjust.htm

Home Office (1999) *Inter-departmental Circular on Establishing Youth Offending Teams.* London: Home Office.

Home Office (2001) *Final Warning Scheme: Further Guidance for the Police and YOTs.* London: Home Office and Youth Justice Board.

Home Office (2002a) *Narrowing the Justice Gap, Framework Document.* http://www.homeoffice.gov.uk/justice/justicegap.html

Home Office (2002b) *Justice for All: Responses to the Auld and Halliday Reports.* Cmd. 5563. London: HMSO.

Home Office (2003) *Every Child Matters.* Cmd. 5860. London: Stationery Office.

Hoyle, C., Young, R. and Hill, R. (2001) *Proceed with Caution: An Evaluation of the Thames Valley Police Initiative in Restorative Cautioning.* York: Joseph Rowntree Foundation.

Hoyle, C. (2002) Securing Restorative Justice for the Non-Participating Victim, in Hoyle, C. and Young, R. (eds.) *New Visions of Crime Victims.* Oxford: Hart Publishing.

Jennings, D. (2003) *One Year Juvenile Reconviction Rates: First Quarter of 2001 Cohort.* Home Office Online Report 18/03, http://www.homeoffice.gov.uk/rds

Jones, D. (1996) Tough on Crime and Nasty to Children. *Prison Report.* 36: 4-5.

Kemp, V., Sorsby, A. Liddle, M., et al. (2002) *Assessing Responses to Youth Offending in Northamptonshire.* London: Nacro.

Kershaw, C. (1999) Interpreting Reconviction Rates, in Brogden, M. (ed.) *The British Criminology Conferences: Selected Proceedings.* 2. http://www.britsoccrim.org/bccsp/vol02/05KERSH.HTM

Kirk, J. and Reid, G. (2001) An Examination of the Relationship between Dyslexia and Offending in Young People and the Implications for the Training System. *Dyslexia Journal.* 7.

Liddle, M. and Gelsthorpe, L. (1994) *Inter-Agency Crime Prevention Papers.* Police Research Group Briefing Note. London: Home Office.

Lipsey, M.W. and Wilson, D.B. (1998) Effective Interventions for Serious Juvenile Offenders, in Loeber, R. and Farrington, D.P. (eds.) *Serious and Violent Juvenile Offenders: Risk Factors and Successful Interventions.* Thousand Oaks: Sage.

Maruna, S. (2000) Desistance From Crime and Offender Rehabilitation: A Tale of Two Research Literatures. *Offender Programs Report.* 4: 1, 5-9.

McGuire, J. (2000) *PLUS+ Programme Manual.* Liverpool: University of Liverpool.

McNeill, F. and Bachelor, S. (2002) Chaos, Containment and Change. *Youth Justice.* 2: 1, 27-43.

Moffitt, T. (1993) Adolescent-limited and Life-Course Persistent Anti-Social Behaviour: A Developmental Taxonomy. *Psychological Review.* 100: 674-701.

Moore, R. (2004) Intensive Supervision and Surveillance Programmes for Young Offenders: The Evidence-Base so Far, in Burnett, R. and Roberts, C. (eds.) *Evidence-Based Practice in Probation and Youth Justice.* Cullompton: Willan.

Muncie, J. (2001) A New Deal for Youth? Early Intervention and Correctionalism, in Hughes, G., McLaughlin, E. and Muncie, J. (eds.) *Crime Prevention and Community Safety: New Directions.* London: Sage.

NACRO (1998) *Diverting Young People from Crime: A Guide Based on Northamptonshire's Experience of Working in Partnership.* London: Nacro.

NACRO (2003) *A Failure of Justice: Reducing Child Imprisonment.* London: Nacro.

Newburn, T. (2002) Young People, Crime, and Youth Justice, in Maguire, M., Morgan, R. and Reiner, R. (eds.) *The Oxford Handbook of Criminology.* 3rd edn. Oxford: Oxford University Press.

Newburn, T., Crawford, A., Earle, R., et al. (2002*) The Introduction of Referral Orders into the Youth Justice System: Final Report.* Home Office Research Study 242. London: Home Office Research, Development and Statistics Directorate.

Newman, R. (2001) Numeracy and Literacy: The Way Forward. *Youth Justice Board News.* 8: 12.

Pearson, G. (1983) *Hooligan: A History of Respectable Fears.* London: Macmillan.

Pearson, G., Blagg, H., Smith, D., et al. (1992) Crime, Community and Conflict: The Multi-Agency Approach, in Downes, D. (ed.) *Unravelling Criminal Justice.* Basingstoke: Macmillan.

Perfect, M. (2000) Regional Meetings Applaud Improvements. *Youth Justice Board News.* 6: 2.

Perfect, M. (2003) A Clear and Consistent Direction. *Youth Justice Board News.* 17: 7.

Performance and Innovation Unit (2000) *Wiring it up: Whitehall's Management of Cross-Cutting Policies and Services.* London: Cabinet Office.

Phillips, C., Jacobson, J., Prime, R., et al. (2002) *Crime and Disorder Reduction Partnerships: Round One Progress.* Police Research Series, Paper 151. London: Home Office.

Pitkeathley, R. (2000) Joined-up Working Makes YOT Partnerships an 'Unqualified

Success'. *Youth Justice Board News.* 6: 1.

Pitts, J. (1998) Dear Jack Straw. *Criminal Justice Matters,* 31: 20.

Pitts, J. (2000) The New Youth Justice and the Politics of Electoral Anxiety, in Goldson, B. (ed.) *The New Youth Justice.* Lyme Regis: Russell House Publishing.

Pitts, J. (2001) Korrectional Karaoke: New Labour and the Zombification of Youth Justice. *Youth Justice.* 1: 2, 3-16.

Pitts, J. (2003) *The New Politics of Youth Crime,* Revised edn. Lyme Regis: Russell House Publishing.

Prison Reform Trust (2001) *Troubled Inside: Responding to the Mental Health Needs of Children and Young People in Prison.* London: Prison Reform Trust.

Ramsbotham, Sir David (2001) Reflections of a Chief Inspector. *Youth Justice.* 1: 1, 17-27.

Roberts, C., Baker, K., Merrington, S., et al. (2001) *Validity and Reliability of Asset: Interim Report to the Youth Justice Board.* Oxford: Centre for Criminological Research.

Robinson, G. and McNeill, F. (2003) Purposes Matter: Examining the 'Ends' of Probation, in Mair, G. (ed.) *What Matters in Probation?* Cullompton: Willan.

Rutherford, A. (1993) *Criminal Justice and the Pursuit of Decency.* Oxford: Oxford University Press.

Rutherford, A. (1985) *Growing Out of Crime.* London: Penguin.

Rutter, M., Giller, M. and Hagell, A. (1998) *Antisocial Behavior by Young People.* Cambridge: Cambridge University Press.

Schweinhart, L., Barnes, H. and Weikart, D. (1993) *Significant Benefits: The High/Scope Perry Preschool Study Through Age 27.* Ypsilanti: High/Scope Press.

Shapland, J., Hibbert, J., l'Anson, J., et al. (1995) *Milton Keynes Criminal Justice Audit.* Sheffield: University of Sheffield Institute for the Study of the Legal Profession.

Simmons, J. and Dodd, T. (eds.) (2003) *Crime in England and Wales 2002/2003.* London: Home Office Communication Development Unit.

Smith, D. (2000) Corporatism and the New Youth Justice, in Goldson, B. (ed.) *The New Youth Justice.* Lyme Regis: Russell House Publishing.

Smith, R.S. (2003) *Youth Justice: Ideas, Policy, Practice.* Cullompton: Willan.

Stake, R.E. (2000) The Case Study Method in Social Inquiry, in Gomm, R., Hammersley, M. and Foster, P. (eds.) *Case Study Method: Key Issues, Key Texts.* London: Sage.

Tarling, R. (1993) *Analysing Offending: Data, Models and Interpretations.* London: HMSO.

Tarling, R., Burrows, J. and Clarke, A. (2001) *Dalston Youth Project, Part II: An Evaluation.* Research Study 232. London: Home Office.

Utting, D. and Vennard, J. (2000) *What Works with Young Offenders in the Community.* Ilford: Barnardo's.

Von Hirsch, A. (2001) Proportionate Sentences for Juveniles: How Different Than for Adults? *Punishment and Society.* 3: 221-36.

Warner, Lord Norman (2003) Let the Punishment Fit the Crime. *Youth Justice Board News.* 16: 11.

Waters, I., Moore, R., Roberts, C., et al. (2003) *Intensive Supervision and Surveillance Programmes for Persistent Young Offenders in England and Wales: Interim Report to the Youth Justice Board.* Oxford: University of Oxford Centre for Criminological Research.

Weijers, I. (2002) The Moral Dialogue: A Pedagogical Perspective on Juvenile Justice, in Weijers, I. and Duff, A. (eds.) *Punishing Juveniles: Principle and Critique.* Oxford: Hart.

West, D.J. (1982) *Delinquency: Its Roots, Careers and Prospects.* London: Heinemann.

Wilcox, A. (2003) Evidence-based Youth Justice? Some Valuable Lessons From an Evaluation for the Youth Justice Board. *Youth Justice.* 3: 1, 19-33.

Wilcox, A. with Hoyle, C. (2002) *Final Report for the Youth Justice Board on the National*

Evaluation of Restorative Justice Projects. Oxford: Centre for Criminological Research.

Wright, C. (2003) Good Performance Gets the Green Light. *Youth Justice Board News.* 17: 5.

Young, K. (1999) *The Art of Youth Work.* Lyme Regis: Russell House Publishing.

Youth Justice Board (1999) *Annual Report and Accounts 1999.* London: YJB.

Youth Justice Board (2001a) *Risk and Protective Factors Associated with Youth crime and Effective Interventions to Prevent it: Research undertaken by Communities that Care on behalf of the Youth Justice Board.* London: YJB.

Youth Justice Board (June 2001b) Putting Something Back. *Youth Justice Board News.* 3: 1.

Youth Justice Board (2001c) *The Preliminary Report on the Operation of the New Youth Justice System.* London: YJB.

Youth Justice Board (2001d) *Guidance for Youth Offending Teams on Achieving Equality.* London: YJB.

Youth Justice Board (2002) *Building on Success: Youth Justice Board Review 2001/2002.* London: YJB.

Youth Justice Board (2003*) Gaining Ground in the Community: Annual Review 2002/2003.* London: YJB.

Zimring, F.E. (2000) Penal Proportionality for the Young Offender: Notes on Immaturity, Capacity, and Diminished Responsibility, in Grisso, T. and Schwartz, R.G. (eds.) *Youth on Trial: A Developmental Perspective on Juvenile Justice.* Chicago: University of Chicago Press.

Index

last date

2